Handmade Giftwrap, Bows, Cards & Tags

Handmade Giftwrap, Bows, Cards & Tags

Jill Williams Grover

Sterling Publishing Co, Inc.,
New York
A Sterling/Chapelle Book

Chapelle Ltd.

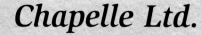

Owner: Jo Packham

Editor: Linda Orton

Staff: Marie Barber, Ann Bear, Areta Bingham,
Kass Burchett, Rebecca Christensen, Dana Durney,
Marilyn Goff, Holly Hollingsworth, Susan Jorgensen,
Barbara Milburn, Karmen Quinney, Leslie Ridenour,
Cindy Stoeckl, Gina Swapp

Photography: Kevin Dilley, photographer for Hazen Photography

Photo Stylist: Jo Packham

Designers: Areta Bingham, Holly Fuller, Jill Grover, Laci, Levi, and
River Grover, Amber Hansen, Michelle Thompson, Ann Williams

Acknowledgements: DecoArt Americana

Library of Congress Cataloging-in-Publication Data

Grover, Jill Williams.
    Handmade giftwrap, bows, cards & tags / Jill Williams Grover.
       p.   cm.
    "A Sterling/Chapelle book."
    Includes index.
    ISBN 0-8069-5793-X
    1. Paper work. 2. Gift wrapping. 3. Greeting cards. I. Title
  TT870.G797 1999
  745.54--dc21   99-32329
                                      CIP

10 9 8 7 6 5 4 3 2 1

A Sterling/Chapelle Book

Published by Sterling Publishing Company, Inc.
387 Park Avenue South, New York, NY 10016
© 1999 by Chapelle Ltd.
Distributed in Canada by Sterling Publishing
℅ Canadian Manda Group, One Atlantic Avenue, Suite 105
Toronto, Ontario, Canada M6K 3E7
Distributed in Great Britain and Europe by Cassell PLC
Wellington House, 125 Strand, London WC2R 0BB, England
Distributed in Australia by Capricorn Link (Australia) Pty Ltd.
P.O. Box 6651, Baulkham Hills, Business Centre, NSW 2153, Australia
Printed in China
All Rights Reserved

Sterling ISBN 0-8069-5793-X

If you have any questions or comments, please contact:

Chapelle Ltd., Inc.
P.O. Box 9252
Ogden, UT 84409

Phone: (801) 621-2777
FAX: (801) 621-2788
e-mail: Chapelle@aol.com

Jill Grover works as an Interior Designer, and is the author of *Scary Scenes for Halloween*. She resides with her family in Northern Utah.

This book is dedicated to my mom
who taught me to believe . . . .

Table of Contents

1 *Introduction*

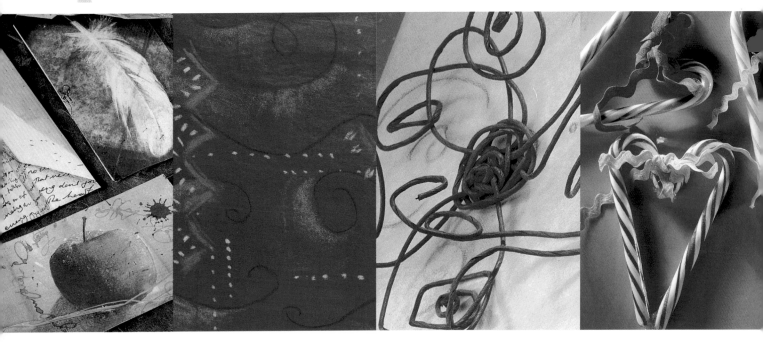

Gifts are purchased with someone special in mind. The same effort that goes into the selection of a gift should go into the wrap, trim, tag, or card.

Christmas, birthday, wedding, and all-occasion gifts deserve better than the simple purchase of matching paper, ribbon, and card.

If you are looking to personalize a gift and add that creative touch, this book will give you ideas as well as step-by-step instructions.

General Instructions 2

Measuring & Cutting Wrap

materials:

Ruler or tape measure
Scissors: craft
Wrapping paper

2. Lay box flat on paper and roll across paper three times, adding 2" overlap.

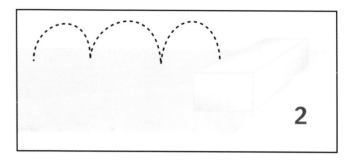

instructions:

1. Lay wrapping paper on flat surface. Using ruler, measure depth of box. Place top of box ⅔ of depth dimension below paper edge. Allow same dimension for opposite end of paper.

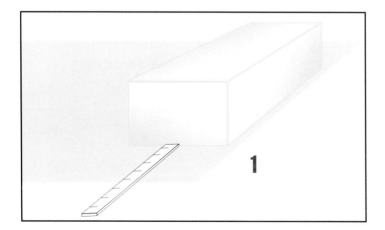

3. Using scissors, cut wrapping paper to measurements.

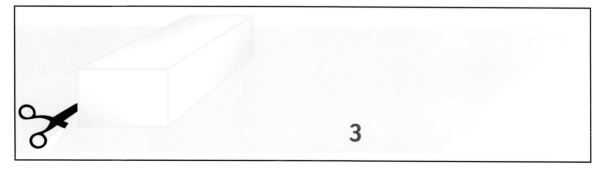

Wrapping Box Ends

Method One

materials:

Double-sided tape (optional)
Transparent tape
Wrapping paper

instructions:

1. Wrap sides of box with wrapping paper and secure with tape. With seam side up, crease and fold down top edge of paper. Secure with tape.

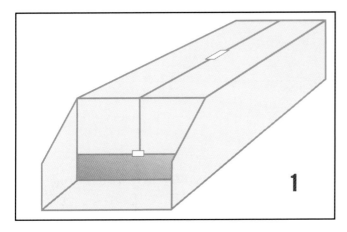

2. Holding top flap in place with one hand, crease and fold in one side end flap.

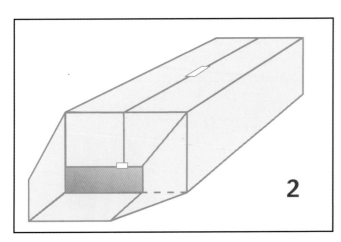

3. Holding folded side end flap in place, crease and fold in remaining side end flap.

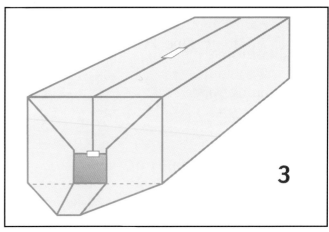

4. Crease and fold up bottom end flap. Tape in place. *Note: Double-sided tape may be used on inside of flap.*

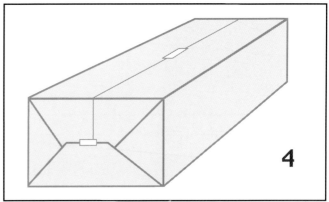

Method Two

materials:

Double-sided tape (optional)
Transparent tape
Wrapping paper

2. Crease and fold down top end flap.

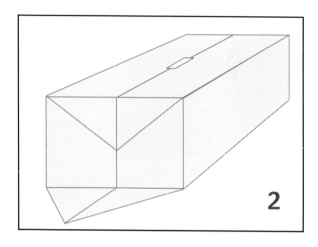

instructions:

1. Wrap sides of box with wrapping paper and secure with tape. With seam side up, crease and fold in side flaps. Crease top and bottom end flaps, making triangles.

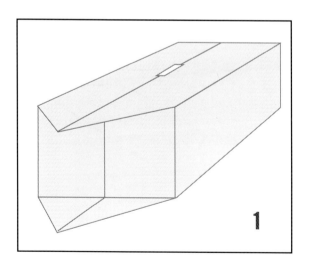

3. Crease and fold up bottom end flap. Secure with tape. *Option: Double-sided tape may be used on inside of flap.*

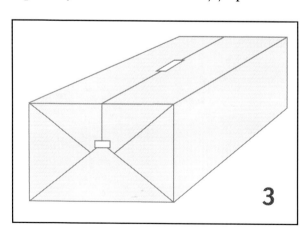

Wrapping Round Boxes

materials:

Construction paper
Craft glue
Scissors: craft; decorative-edged (optional)
Transparent tape
Wrapping paper

instructions:

1. Using craft scissors, cut wrapping paper so that side edges will fold to center of box. Cut off corners of paper.

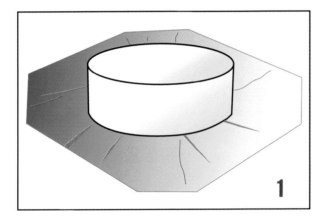

2. Place box topside down on center of wrapping paper. Pull one corner tightly to center of box. Secure with tape.

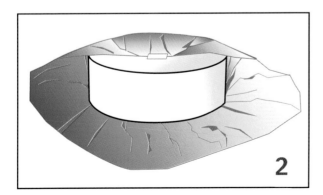

3. Pull next edge up, folding and pulling to center. Secure with tape. Repeat, going around box until all edges are folded and pulled to center.

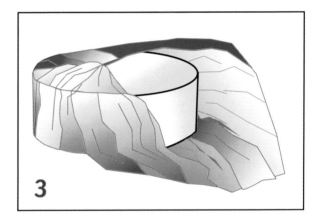

4. Cut out circle from construction paper that is ¼" smaller than bottom of box. *Option: Decorative-edged scissors may be used.* Center paper circle over taped end of box and adhere with glue to hide edges.

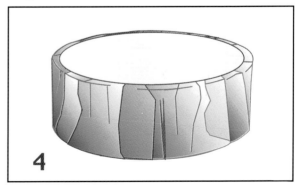

Wrapping Ribbon

materials:

Ribbon

instructions:

1. Drape ribbon over top of gift.

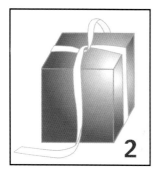

2. Turn gift and ribbon upside down and pull ribbon tight. Twist ribbon ends around each other and pull down opposite sides.

3. Turn gift right side up and pull ribbon tight. Slide ribbon ends under ribbon. Tie ribbon in knot to secure. Tie ribbon as desired.

Scoring & Folding Card Stock

When using card stock and heavier-weight papers, scoring will give folded edges a more professional look.

materials:

Bone folder or stylus
Craft knife or paper cutter (optional)
Pencil
Ruler

instructions:

1. Using ruler and pencil, lightly mark the center or area to be folded.

2. Place ruler edge on pencil mark, and using bone folder or stylus, press a line following mark as shown in Illustration A.

3. The score mark becomes the outside of fold. Carefully fold paper aligning edges. Use roller side of bone folder or side of stylus to smooth and flatten fold.

4. Using craft knife and ruler or paper cutter, trim any folded edges that do not match properly.

A

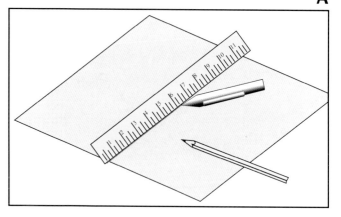

3 *Buy & Wrap*

Pastels & Crepe

materials:

Butcher paper: pastels
Crepe paper
Fabric-covered hearts
Hot-glue gun and glue sticks
Paper lace
Ribbon: sheer
Scissors: craft
Silk florals and fruits: pastels

instructions:

One
Wrap gift in butcher paper. Wrap ribbon around gift and knot. Place floral stem on top of knot and tie bow to secure. Using hot-glue gun, adhere heart.

Two
Wrap gift in butcher paper. Wrap paper lace horizontally around gift. Wrap ribbon around paper lace horizontally and tie bow to secure.

Three
Wrap gift in crepe paper. Wrap ribbon around box and tie bow to secure. Using craft scissors, cut two additional lengths of ribbon. Tie ribbon with one length of ribbon offset from first bow. Repeat with remaining ribbon. Using hot-glue gun, adhere fruit to top of gift as desired.

Touch of Class

materials:

Cording (to match tiebacks)
Drapery tieback tassels
Kraft© paper
Lace-edged handkerchief
Ornament cross
Ribbon: sheer; wire-edged sheer
Scissors: craft
Wrapping paper

instructions:

One
Wrap box with wrapping paper. Wrap wire-edged ribbon around gift and knot to secure. Attach ornament. Using craft scissors, cut five lengths of ribbon long enough to tie a bow. Tie bow with one length of ribbon. Tie next bow in opposite direction. Repeat with remaining ribbon pieces.

Two

Wrap gift with Kraft paper. Wrap cording around box and secure in back. Thread curtain tieback tassels under cording in front. Tie triple knot as shown in Illustration A.

Three

Wrap gift with Kraft paper. Drape handkerchief on gift. Wrap sheer ribbon around gift and tie bow to secure.

A

Harvest

materials:

Drapery tieback tassels
Fresh leaf or leaf stamp
Handmade paper
Mulberry paper
Paintbrushes
Plant pod
Ribbon: sheer
Watercolor paints

instructions:

One

Using paintbrush, paint leaf
or leaf stamp with paints.
Stamp leaf on mulberry paper.
Allow to dry. Tear leaf from
mulberry paper. Wrap tassels
around gift and tie. Attach
leaf artwork to gift.

Two

Using paintbrush, paint
plant pod to match hand-
made paper with paints.
Allow to dry. Wrap box
with handmade paper.
Wrap ribbon around gift
and knot to secure. Wrap
tassels around gift and knot
as shown in Illustration A.
Slide dried pod through
tassel knot.

A

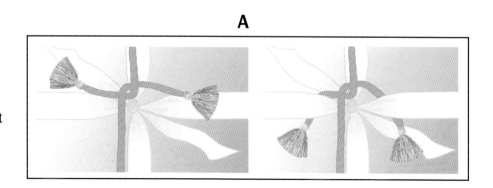

One

Wrap package with wrapping paper. Separate top layer of napkin from back. Discard back. Tear or cut napkin. Adhere napkin to top of package as desired. Thread beads on three lengths of wire as desired. Loosely twist wire strand and beads together. Wrap box with beaded wire, beginning in back. Wrap wire ends together at back of gift to secure.

Treasures

materials:

Beads: assorted
Decorative paper napkins
Pine cone: gold
Ribbon: gold-edged sheer;
    wire-edged metallic web;
    wire-edged sheer
Tissue paper
Wire: small-gauge
Wrapping paper

Two

Wrap gift with wrapping paper. Tie gold-edged ribbon around gift and knot, leaving 42" tails. Tie bow as shown in Illustration A. Tie second bow offset from first bow. Tie third bow offset from first two bows.

A

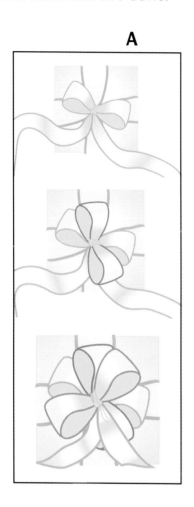

Three

Wrap gift with tissue paper. Wrap web ribbon around box and knot to secure. Attach pine cone. Attach four varying lengths of wire-edged sheer ribbon to web ribbon and tie bow.

One

Wrap gift in Kraft paper.
Wrap gift horizontally with
burlap ribbon, overlapping in
back. Wrap cinamay ribbon
around gift horizontally and
tie bow to secure.

Two

Wrap gift with tissue paper.
Wrap metallic ribbon around
gift and knot to secure. Make
three loops with ribbon and
using hot glue, adhere ribbon loops to center of gift.
Adhere leaves and glitter
ornaments to center of gift.
Adhere rose to center of gift
arranging leaves, ornaments,
and ribbon loops as desired.

Copper

materials:

Bird
Glitter ornaments
Handmade paper
Hand-painted paper
Hot-glue gun and glue sticks
Kraft© paper
Mulberry paper
Ribbon: cinamay (two colors); sheer;
    wire-edged burlap; wire-edged metallic
Satin rose
Silk handkerchief
Silk leaves
Tissue paper
Wire: small gauge

Three

Wrap gift with handmade
paper. Wrap metallic ribbon
around package and tie bow.

Four

Wrap gift with mulberry
paper. Wrap sheer ribbon
around gift horizontally
and secure with tape in
back. Wrap ribbon around
gift vertically and secure in
back. Tie bow and using
hot-glue gun, adhere to
front of gift.

5

2

3

4

1

6

Six

Place gift in center of silk handkerchief. Pull corners up and tie in knot as shown in Illustration B. Tuck ends under and pull up remaining corners and knot.

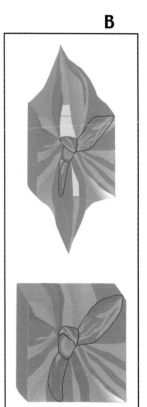

B

Five

Wrap gift with hand-painted paper. Wrap cinamay ribbon around gift and knot to secure. Make bow as shown in Illustration A, using cinamay ribbon and wire. Wire bow to knot. Attach bird with wire.

A

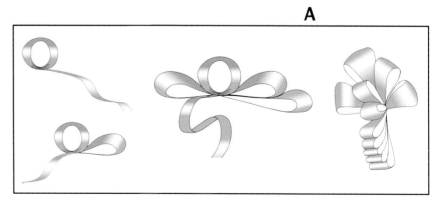

23

Nature

Fabric
Handmade papers
Hot-glue gun and glue sticks
Mulberry paper: two colors
Needlepoint yarn
Raffia
Ribbon: wire-edged metallic;
   ⅛" metallic
Scissors: craft
Twigs (5)

One
Tear one color of mulberry paper to go around gift lengthwise. Tear second color of mulberry paper to go around box width-wise. Wrap papers around gift as shown in photograph. Wrap several lengths of raffia around gift and knot to secure.

Two

Wrap gift with handmade paper. Wrap ⅛" ribbon around gift, knotting in back to secure. Make star from twigs as shown in photograph, Connect twigs by wrapping with ⅛" ribbon and knotting to secure. Using hot-glue gun, adhere star to front of gift.

Three

Wrap gift with fabric. Wrap with four lengths of yarn and knot to secure. Using scissors, cut forty lengths of yarn long enough to tie a bow. Tie bow to package.

Four

Wrap gift with handmade paper. Twist metallic ribbon and wrap around gift one direction. Knot to secure. Tie shamrock bow with metallic ribbon as shown in Illustration A. Using hot-glue gun, adhere bow to top of gift.

A

One

Place gift in cardboard container. Using hot-glue gun, adhere silk vine and berries to top of container.

Two

Wrap gift in Kraft paper. Wrap sheer ribbon around box and tie in bow. Using craft scissors, cut four lengths of ribbon long enough to tie a bow. Tie bow with one ribbon. Tie next bow opposite direction. Repeat with remaining ribbon pieces. Attach paper roses to center of bow.

Three

Wrap gift in Kraft paper. Adhere paper ribbon rose to center of gift.

Four

Place gift in cardboard container. Wrap pine garland around gift and twist together to secure. Using hot-glue gun, adhere leaves and berries to center of gift. Curl pine garland as desired.

Brown Paper

materials:

Button: wooden
Cardboard containers
Découpage medium
Fabric
Hot-glue gun and glue sticks
Kraft© paper
Paintbrush
Paper ribbon rose
Paper roses
Papier-mâché box
Pearl cotton
Ribbon: sheer
Scissors: craft; pinking shears
Silk berries, leaves, pine garland, vine

Five

Using pinking shears, cut fabric ¼" smaller than papier-mâché box lid. Using paintbrush, apply découpage to top of box lid. Center fabric on box lid. Allow to dry. Apply découpage to top and sides of box lid. Allow to dry. Using hot-glue gun, adhere button to center of box lid. Tie bow using two lengths of pearl cotton. Adhere to button.

Colors of
Nature

materials:

Bird
Colored papers
Cording
Florals: silk and dried
Hot-glue gun and glue sticks
Nest
Ribbon trims
Scissors: craft
Seashells

instructions:

One

Wrap gift in paper. Wrap ribbon trim around gift and tie bow. Cut second length of ribbon trim long enough to tie a bow. Tie next bow opposite direction. Using hot-glue gun, adhere florals, bird, and nest to top of gift.

Two

Wrap gift in paper. Wrap cording around gift and knot to secure. Place florals on top of knot and tie bow to secure. Using hot-glue gun, adhere additional florals and shells to gift as desired.

Three

Wrap gift in paper. Wrap ribbon trim around box and knot to secure. Using craft scissors, cut several lengths of trim long enough to tie a bow. Tie bow around stems of florals to secure.

It's Elementary

materials:

Fabric: plaid; solid
Hand-lettered school paper
Handmade paper
Hot-glue gun and glue sticks
Licorice rope
Pipe cleaners: red (2); white (2)
Raffia
Ribbon: grosgrain; wire-edged cotton
Stuffed toy

instructions:

One

Wrap gift in handmade paper. Wrap grosgrain ribbon around box and knot. Twist red and white pipe cleaners together and bend in shape of candy canes. Repeat with remaining pipe cleaners. Place candy canes on top of knot, facing opposite directions. Tie bow to secure candy canes.

Two
Wrap gift in solid fabric. Wrap strands of raffia around gift and tie in bow. Tuck stuffed toy under raffia.

Three
Wrap gift in solid fabric. Tear plaid fabric into strip. Wrap strip around package and knot.

Four
Wrap gift in hand-lettered paper. Wrap licorice rope around gift and knot.

One

Wrap gift in wrapping paper. Wrap five lengths of string, one of each color, around gift and tie bow to secure. Tie second bow offset, on top of first bow with five additional lengths of string.

For Fun

materials:

Cotton string: five bright colors
Curling ribbon: two colors
Hot-glue gun and glue sticks
Party favor balloons
Pipe cleaners: (3) metallic colors
Press-on bows (4) two of each color
Ribbon: ⅛" satin; polka dot satin;
   wire-edged satin
Wrapping paper: brightly colored

Two

Wrap gift in wrapping paper. Wrap polka dot ribbon around gift and knot to secure. Make bow as shown in Illustration A on page 23. Wire balloons to center of bow. Attach bow to package. Make two ribbon balls from wire-edged ribbon and one from polka dot ribbon as shown in Illustration A. Tie knot with ⅛" ribbon to secure. Using hot-glue gun, adhere to gift around bow.

A

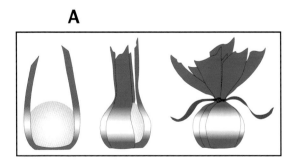

Three

Wrap gift in wrapping paper. Wrap curling ribbon around gift and knot to secure. Place press-on bows on gift. Cut additional lengths of ribbon and curl. Thread ribbon in and out of bows as desired.

Four

Wrap gift in wrapping paper. Wrap one color of curling ribbon around gift and knot to secure. Curl multiple lengths of two colors to make bow desired size. Place bow of curling ribbon under curling ribbon on gift and arrange. Curl pipe cleaners and arrange in ribbon.

Jumbo

Curling ribbon
Disposable plastic
    tablecloth
Fabric: moiré
    satin
Ornament: large
Scissors: fabric

instructions:

One

Wrap gift in tablecloth. Using scissors, cut strip of fabric for ribbon. Wrap fabric around gift and tie in bow. Curl several strands of curling ribbon. Tie ornament to gift with curling ribbon.

Two

Wrap gift in tablecloth. Cut two strips of fabric for ribbon. Wrap one strip of fabric around box horizontally and knot in center of box to secure. Wrap second strip around gift vertically; knot directly over first knot and arrange. Curl several strands of curling ribbon. Tie ornament to gift with curling ribbon.

Sketches

materials:

Adhesive spray
Postal tag
Raffia
Scissors: craft
Wrapping paper

instructions:

1. Using scissors, cut wrapping paper slightly larger than postal tag. Spray one side of postal tag with adhesive. Adhere sticky side of tag to back side of wrapping paper and press to secure. Trim excess paper from around tag.

2. Thread raffia through hole and tie.

Fossil Leaf

materials:

Hot-glue gun and glue sticks
Leaf skeleton
Watercolor paper

instructions:

1. Fold watercolor paper in half lengthwise. Using hot-glue gun, place tiny dab of glue on each end of leaf spine. Adhere leaf to card as desired.

Seasons

materials:

Acrylic paints: three colors
Brayer
Cover-weight art paper
Disposable pallet
Glue stick
Handmade or petal paper
Leaf stamp or fresh leaf
Mulberry (optional)

instructions:

1. Tear rectangle from handmade or petal paper 1⅜" smaller than folded dimensions of card.

2. Place small amount of each paint color on pallet. Using brayer, roll paint colors together, mixing lightly. Roll brayer over stamp surface. Stamp leaf onto handmade or petal paper. Allow to dry.

3. Fold art paper in half lengthwise. *Option: Tear rectangle from mulberry paper ⅜" smaller than folded dimensions of card. Using glue stick, center and adhere mulberry paper to art paper.*

4. Center and using glue stick, adhere leaf to front of card.

Snowman

materials:

Adhesive spray
Card stock: black
Colored papers: green; red;
   white
Glitter powder: white
Glue stick
Graphite paper
Opaque markers: black; white
Pencil
Scissors: craft
Tracing paper

instructions:

1. Using pencil, trace Snowman Patterns onto tracing paper. Place patterns over graphite paper and transfer onto colored paper. Using scissors, cut out snowman pieces. Using black marker, draw face and buttons on snowman.

2. Spray snowman body with adhesive. Sprinkle glitter powder over adhesive.

3. Fold card stock in half. Using glue stick, adhere snowman, hat, and scarf to front of card. Using white marker, write "In the meadow we can build a." Dot marker randomly on card for falling snow.

Hat pattern

Snowman Patterns

Snowman pattern

Scarf pattern

Glossy Tags

materials:

Colorful diecut gift tag
Glaze: glossy
Glitter mesh
Paintbrush
Raffia
Scissors: craft

instructions:

1. Using paintbrush, paint glaze on top side of gift tag. Allow to dry.

2. Using scissors, cut square of glitter mesh large enough to cover tag. Gather and tie at top with piece of raffia.

Child Art

materials:

Child's artwork

instructions:

1. Determine size, and color photocopy child's artwork to fit on bottom half of paper. Fold paper in half with artwork on outside to make card.

Dot-to-Dot

Card stock
Opaque paint markers

1. Fold card stock in half. Using paint markers, paint different sizes and colors of dots on front of card stock. Connect dots to make words or designs.

Brrr!

Adhesive spray
Fabric with rectangular
    design
Postal tags
Ribbon
Scissors: fabric

1. Using scissors, cut out fabric design.

2. Spray back of fabric with adhesive. Press fabric onto postal tags. Thread ribbon through hole and tie.

Hearts & Stars

* Size of hearts and stars on example are for oversized packages. Smaller sizes may be used for smaller gifts.

materials:

Acrylic paints
Drill and drill bits
Needlenose pliers
Paintbrush
Permanent marker
Sandpaper
Wire: medium-gauge
Wire cutters
* Wooden heart: 11" (on example)
* Wooden star: 8" (on example)

instructions:

1. Using paintbrush, paint heart and star with acrylic paints. Allow to dry. Sand edges of heart and star.

2. Using drill and drill bit, drill two holes in top of heart and star. Using wire cutters, cut length of wire. Thread one end of wire through one hole. Using needlenose pliers, bend wire back and twist to secure. Repeat with other side. Using marker, write name on wood. *Note: Write a wish or promise for the recipient on backside of tag.*

materials:

Frosted glass ornament
Metallic marker

instructions:

1. Using metallic marker, write name on ornament.

Spool of Love

materials:

Antique spool
Calligraphy pen
Cording: metallic
Craft glue
Craft wedding rings: (2) (optional)
Mulberry paper
Scissors: craft

instructions:

1. Using scissors, cut paper to fit around inside of spool. Using calligraphy pen, write message on paper.

2. Adhere end of paper to spool with glue. Allow to dry. Wind paper around spool and tie with cording.

3. *Option: Spread ends of one ring apart, place remaining ring over one end and close ring so that rings are interlocked. Attach one ring to cording with knot.*

Gold Leaf

Cording: gold
Découpage medium
Gold leafing
Leafing adhesive
Matches
Paintbrush
Price tag
Scissors: craft
Sealing wax
Specialty paper: sheer
Wax stamp

instructions:

1. Tear a small irregular shape from specialty paper. Using paintbrush, apply small amount of découpage medium on center of tag. Place specialty paper on découpage medium and press into place, allowing paper to wrinkle and fold. Allow to dry. Apply coat of découpage medium over specialty paper and tag surface. Allow to dry.

2. Apply leafing adhesive and gold leafing around edges of tag, following manufacturer's instructions.

3. Using match, melt sealing wax. Drop sealing wax to upper part of tag below hole. Using wax stamp, stamp design into wax. Allow to cool.

4. Using scissors, cut two lengths of gold cord. Thread cords through hole and knot together. Braid cord as desired and tie knot to secure braid.

Glitter Mesh

materials:

Glitter mesh
Hot-glue gun and glue sticks
Scissors: craft
Watercolor paper

instructions:

1. Using scissors, cut gold mesh to same dimensions as watercolor paper. Using hot-glue gun, place tiny dabs of glue on ends of mesh and adhere to outside of watercolor paper. Fold in half.

Dragonfly

materials:

Card stock
Fabric: organza
Glue stick
Metallic marker pen: silver
Paintbrush: large, round
Scissors: fabric
Sewing machine
Thread
Watercolor paints: cobalt
    blue; brown madder (on
    example)
Watercolor paper

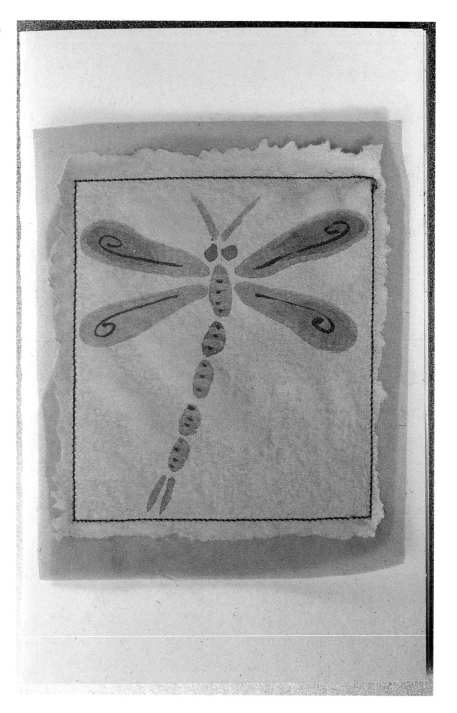

1. Using paintbrush, paint simple dragonfly shape with watercolor paints on watercolor paper. Allow to dry. Using marker pen, outline and shade dragonfly. Allow to dry. Tear paper around dragonfly into a rectangle.

2. Fold card stock in half. Using glue stick, center and adhere dragonfly to front of card. Using scissors, cut rectangle from fabric slightly larger than dragonfly rectangle. Place fabric on dragonfly. Using sewing machine, sew fabric and dragonfly to card.

Lacy

materials:

Craft glue
Decorative card stock
Lace
Photo

1. Fold card stock in half.

2. Photocopy photo, enlarging or reducing as desired. Adhere photocopy to front of card with glue. Place lace on card as desired. Fold raw edges to inside of card and adhere lace to secure.

Antique It

materials:

Decorative card stock
Photo: black-and-white
Photo corners (4)
Shoe polish: ochre
Soft cloth

instructions:

1. Fold card stock in half.

2. Using soft cloth, rub photo with light coat of shoe polish. Mount photo on front of card stock with photo corners.

Lite It

Christmas light bulb
Opaque marker
Pipe cleaner

1. Using marker, write name on bulb.

2. Wrap pipe cleaner around end of bulb and twist. Shape pipe cleaner.

Dye It

Easter egg dye kit
Key tags: white
Marker: fine-line

1. Prepare dye, following manufacturer's instructions. Dip key tags into dye until desired color is achieved. Remove from dye and allow to dry. Using marker, write name on tag.

Pretty In Pink

materials:

Glue stick
Paper: coordinated patterns
    (2); embossed
Paper punch
Ribbon: chiffon
Scissors: craft

instructions:

1. Using glue stick, glue patterned papers with wrong sides together. Allow to dry. Make two vertical folds so the ends of the cards meet in the middle.

2. Using craft scissors, cut embossed paper to inside measurements of card.

3. Using paper punch, punch one hole on each edge of card. Place embossed card with written message inside card. Thread ribbon through holes and tie bow to close card.

1. Fold paper in half horizontally. Turn paper so fold is to the left, then fold in half horizontally again.

2. Using pencil and tracing paper, trace Heart Pattern. Using craft scissors, cut pattern from tracing paper. Using pins, pin pattern to fabric. Using fabric scissors, cut two hearts from fabric.

3. Using sewing machine, sew ³⁄₈" seam around hearts with right sides together, leaving 1" opening. Turn heart right side out through opening. Stuff heart with polyester stuffing. Using needle and thread, hand-stitch heart closed.

4. Cut length of jute and wrap it around heart 2–3 times. Using hot-glue gun, adhere jute ends to back of heart. Adhere heart to front of card. Cut one or more lengths of jute and wrap around card and heart as desired. Adhere jute ends to back or between inside folds of card.

Heart Card

materials:

Fabric
Handmade paper
Hot-glue gun and glue sticks
Jute
Pencil
Polyester stuffing
Scissors: craft; fabric
Sewing needle
Sewing machine
Straight pins
Thread
Tracing paper

Heart Pattern
cut two

opening

Rainbow Trout

Acrylic paints: blue, green, red
Jute ties
Paintbrush: flat
Spray paint
Styrofoam® plate
Wooden fish

1. Place a small amount of each paint color on plate. Add water to paint and mix to obtain an ink-like consistency.

2. Using paintbrush, paint strip of blue along the center of fish lengthwise. Paint green length on outside. Repeat on remaining side with red paint. Allow to dry.

3. Spray jute ties with spray paint. Allow to dry. Tie jute to fish.

Gone Fishing

Acrylic paints
Jute ties
Paintbrush: fine-tip
Sandpaper
Sponge brush
Styrofoam® plate
Toothpick
Wooden fish

1. Place a small amount of each paint color on plate. Using sponge brush, paint desired background color on fish. Allow to dry.

2. Using toothpick for fine dots, and paintbrush for diamonds and swirls, embellish fish as desired. Allow to dry. Using sandpaper, sand edges. Thread jute through hole and knot.

Bubbled Card

materials:

Card stock
Drinking straw
Food coloring
Liquid detergent
Measuring cups
Small container

instructions:

1. In container, mix ½ cup liquid detergent with 1 cup of water. Add a few drops of food coloring to mixture. Using straw, blow into mixture, creating colorful bubbles that come just above the top of the container. Place card stock over the bubbles. As bubbles burst a design will be left. Repeat until desired design is achieved. Allow to dry. *Option: In separate container, mix another color to add second color to card. Allow first color to dry before using second color.*

2. Fold card stock in half with design on outside.

Crackled Tiles

materials:

materials:

Acrylic paints: dk. brown;
   lime green (our example)
Antiquing gel
Crackle medium
Découpage medium
Paintbrushes (3)
Permanent marker
Wooden tile
Wrapping paper motif

instructions:

1. Using paintbrush, paint top and sides of tile with dk. brown paint. Allow to dry. Using paintbrush, apply crackle medium over paint, following manufacturer's instructions. Using paintbrush, paint over crackle medium with lime green paint. Allow to dry.

2. Using paintbrush, apply découpage medium to back of paper motif. Place motif on tile. Apply additional medium over motif smoothing out wrinkles. Allow to dry.

3. Apply thin coat of antiquing gel. Using soft cloth, wipe off any excess gel. Allow to dry.

4. Using marker, write message on back of tile.

Silverware

materials:

Acrylic paint: metallic silver
Old tableware
Paintbrush
Permanent marker:
   medium-point

instructions:

1. Using paintbrush, paint tableware with acrylic paint. Allow to dry. Using marker, write name on tableware.

Posies

Card stock: blue; green; red;
   yellow
Cover-weight art paper
Craft glue
Marker: medium-point (optional)
Scissors: craft
Wrapping paper: tiny polka-dot;
   patterned

1. Fold art paper in half. Using scissors, cut out three stems and four leaves from green card stock. Cut out flowers from remaining piece of card stock. Cut centers for flowers from polka-dot paper. Cut vase from patterned paper.

2. Make slit in upper part of vase to insert flower stems. Apply glue under outside edges of vase and adhere to front of card.

3. Determine placement of stems and flowers. Apply glue to stem and slide bottom end of stem through slit in vase, then press to adhere. Repeat with remaining stems.

4. Adhere flower to top of stem. Repeat for remaining flowers. Adhere polka-dot paper to center of each flower. Adhere one leaf to each outside stem and two to inside stem. *Option: Using marker, write Y-O-U in center of each flower.*

Rooster

Colored papers: blue; red; yellow
Marker: fine-line, black
Polka-dot paper: yellow
Ribbon: yellow polka dot
Scissors: craft
White glue

52

Instructions:

1. Fold blue paper in half. Using scissors, cut polka-dot paper same size as folded dimensions. Adhere polka dot paper to inside of blue paper with thin coat of craft glue.

2. Cut ribbon same length as folded edge of card. Apply strip of glue down folded side of card. Place half of ribbon lengthwise on glue strip and press to adhere. Turn card over and squeeze strip of glue on folded edge down back of card. Fold ribbon over and press to adhere. Allow to dry.

3. Cut egg-shape from polka-dot paper for body. Cut head from red paper. Cut rooster beak from yellow paper. Adhere rooster to front of card.

4. Using fine-line marker, draw rooster eyes, wings, and feet. Outline polka dots on rooster body.

Bugs

materials:

Adhesive spray
Dimensional fabric paint (optional)
Postal tag
Ribbon
Scissors: craft
Wrapping paper

instructions:

1. Using scissors, cut wrapping paper slightly larger than postal tag. Spray one side of postal tag with adhesive. Adhere sticky side of tag to back side of wrapping paper and press to secure. Trim excess paper from around tag.

2. *Option: Apply fabric paint as desired.*

3. Thread ribbon through hole and tie.

5 *Bows & Trims*

Napkin Bow

materials:

Hot-glue gun and
  glue sticks
Napkin ring
Paper dinner napkins:
  decorative (2)

instructions:

1. Open up napkins and lay flat, decorative side up. Pick up napkin from center and slide center through napkin ring. Repeat with second napkin. Fan out to make bow.

2. Using hot-glue gun, adhere napkins to inside of napkin ring. Adhere ring to gift.

Woven Web

materials:

Charm
Craft glue
Gold wire: fine gauge
Needlenose pliers
Wire cutters
Wrapped giftbox

instructions:

1. Using wire cutters, cut long length of wire. Make wire loop large enough to fit over one corner of gift. Wrap wire back and forth around giftbox looping wire through other wire strands to create a web effect. When wrapping is complete, tie wire off to secure.

2. Using craft glue, glue charm as desired to gift.

materials:

Needlenose pliers
Wire cutters
Wire: small gauge
Wrapped gift

instructions:

1. Using wire cutters, cut two lengths of wire long enough to wrap around gift in both directions plus 4".

2. Wrap wire around center front of gift to back. Using needlenose pliers, twist wires ½ turn on center back of gift. Wrap wires opposite direction to front center of gift. Twist wires three times. Press wire into a circular knot. Trim off excess wire.

Wire & Leaf

materials:

Beads: leaf (4); oval (2)
Gold wire: small gauge
Needlenose pliers
Wire cutters

instructions:

1. Using wire cutters, cut length of wire long enough to wrap around gift in both directions plus 4".

2. Wrap wire around center front of gift to back. Using needlenose pliers, twist wire ½ turn on center back of gift. Wrap wires opposite direction to front center of gift. Twist wires three times.

3. Place two leaf beads on each wire, twisting wires together once. Place oval bead on each wire. Turn wire back toward bead in hook shape to hold bead in place. Trim off excess wire.

Twinkle Star

materials:

Glitter: gold
Grapevine star
Ribbon
Spray paint: gold

instructions:

1. Using spray paint, spray star. Sprinkle on glitter while paint is still wet. Allow to dry. Tie on ribbon.

Net Bows

materials:

Hot-glue gun and glue sticks
Needle and thread
Ribbon: 6" wide netting (1¼ yd.)
Seashells

instructions:

1. Using needle and thread, sew a running stitch lengthwise down the middle of ribbon. Pull thread ends to gather tightly. Tie ends together.

2. Using hot-glue gun, adhere shell to center of bow. Adhere bow to gift.

Birdhouse

materials:

Acrylic paint: brown; green (on example)
Bay leaves
Birdseed
Hot-glue gun and glue sticks
Paintbrushes
Raffia
Tear-drop ornament: plastic

instructions:

1. Using paintbrush, paint ornament green. Allow to dry. Paint brown circle for door.

2. Using hot glue gun, apply glue around top of door. Adhere birdseed and broken bay leaves. Tie small raffia bow and adhere to bottom of opening. Tie larger bow to ornament hanger.

Tiger Eye

materials:

Button: decorative
Hot-glue gun and glue sticks
Ribbon: sheer, 2 colors
Wire: small gauge

instructions:

1. Make bow as shown in Illustration A on page 23 from one color of ribbon. Make slightly larger bow from remaining color.

2. Place small bow on top of larger bow and wire together with excess wire.

3. Using hot-glue gun, adhere button to center of bow.

Wire Hearts

materials:

materials:

Ribbon: sheer
Spray paint
Wire heart

instructions:

1. Spray heart with spray paint. Allow to dry. Tie on ribbon.

Floral Button

materials:

Acrylic paint
Button: medium, 4 holes
Embroidery floss: 6 strands
Embroidery needle
Hot-glue gun and glue sticks
Paintbrush
Trim: rick-rack
Thread: green

instructions:

1. Using paintbrush and acrylic paint, paint button. Allow to dry.

2. Using needle and thread, stitch stems as shown in photograph. Using needle and embroidery floss, stitch French knot on top hole of button, referring to photograph.

3. Using hot-glue gun, adhere button to center of rick-rack.

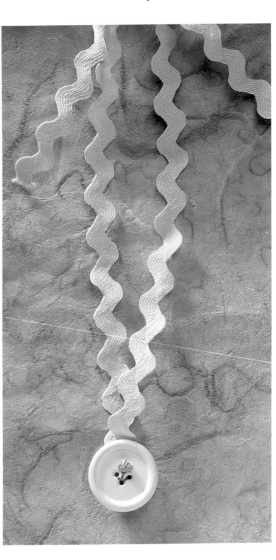

3-d Hearts

materials:

Acrylic paint: metallic
Hot-glue gun and glue sticks
Metallic thread
Paintbrush
Wooden heart: 3-d

instructions:

1. Using paintbrush, paint heart. Allow to dry.

2. Starting at bottom of heart on back side, wrap metallic thread around heart as desired, ending at bottom back of heart.

3. Using hot-glue gun, apply tiny dab of glue on thread ends to secure. Adhere heart to ribbon or gift.

Rusty Ring

materials:

Needlenose pliers
Rusty can top
Rusty wire

instructions:

1. Place wire through rusty can top. Using needlenose pliers, bend wire together to make loop.

Rusty Angel

materials:

Beads
Felt scrap
Hammer
Hot-glue gun and glue sticks
Nail
Needlenose pliers
Rusty tin angel
Scissors: fabric
Wire: small gauge
Wire cutters

instructions:

1. Using fabric scissors, cut felt same size as angel head. Cut several short lengths of wire. Twist wire into small spirals. Using hot-glue gun, adhere one end of spirals to top of felt. Adhere felt to back of angel's head.

2. Using hammer and nail, punch hole in each wing. Using wire cutters, cut length of wire and thread through one hole. Using needlenose pliers, bend wire back and twist to hold. Slide beads onto wire for garland. Thread wire end through other hole, bend back, and twist to hold.

Rusty Stars

materials:

Hardware cloth
Hot-glue gun and glue sticks
Rusty tin stars (2)

instructions:

1. Using hot-glue gun, adhere stars to hardware cloth. Adhere Rusty Stars to gift.

Tin Angel

materials:

Hardware cloth
Hot-glue gun and glue sticks
Spray paint: silver
Tin angel

instructions:

1. Using spray paint, paint angel. Using hot-glue gun, adhere angel to hardware cloth. Adhere Tin Angel to gift.

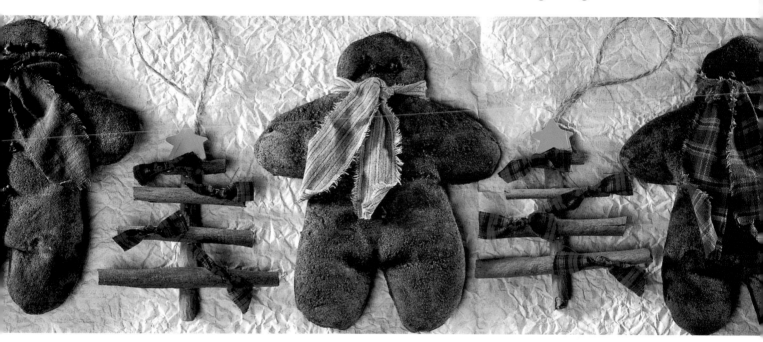

Spice Tree

instructions:

1. Using hot-glue gun, adhere cinnamon sticks together as shown in photograph, using shortest for top and longest for bottom and trunk. Adhere loop of jute to top of tree.

materials:

Acrylic paint: yellow
Cinnamon sticks (5)
Fabric
Gingerbread man
Hot-glue gun and glue sticks
Jute
Paintbrush
Wooden star

2. Using paintbrush, apply paint to star. Allow to dry. Adhere star to top of tree.

3. Tear small strips of fabric. Tie bows, and adhere to branches. Tie strip around neck of gingerbread man and knot. Attach gingerbread man to gift by placing scarf under gift ribbon before knotting.

Snowman Topper

materials:

Acrylic paints: black; pink; white
Buttons: black, small (2)
Crackle medium
Hot-glue gun and glue sticks
Infant elastic-top bootie
Miniature clay pots: graduated
    sizes (3)
Paintbrushes: flat, small (2)
Paper twist: orange
Pom pom: small
Ribbon: wire-edged
Scissors: craft
Twigs (2)

Tree Topper

materials:

Acrylic paints: green; yellow
Crackle medium
Gold wire: small-gauge
Hot-glue gun and glue sticks
Miniature clay pots: graduated
    sizes (3)
Paintbrushes: flat, small (2)
Scissors: craft
Wire cutters
Wooden star

instructions:

1. Using paintbrush, paint clay pots with green. Allow to dry. Using paintbrush, apply crackle medium, following manufacturer's instructions. Paint pots with green. Allow to dry. Paint star with yellow.

2. Using hot-glue gun, adhere pots together, stacking one on top of another, open side down.

3. Using wire cutters, cut a length of wire. Wrap one end around star twice to secure. Coil remaining wire and adhere end of coil to top clay pot inside drainage hole. Adhere bottom of Tree Topper to gift.

1. Using paintbrush, paint clay pots with white paint. Allow to dry. Using paintbrush, apply crackle medium, following manufacturer's instructions. Paint pots with white paint. Allow to dry.

2. Using hot-glue gun, adhere pots together, stacking one on top of another, open side down. Paint cheeks with pink paint. Paint face with black paint.

3. Using craft scissors, cut a small piece of paper twist. Twist one end to point for nose. Adhere opposite end to face. Adhere buttons to center front of middle pot. Adhere twigs in place for arms. Tie ribbon around neck for scarf. Push toe end of bootie inside and adhere pom pom to center. Turn ankle cuff up for brim and adhere bootie to snowman's head. Adhere bottom of Snowman Topper to gift.

Rick-Rack Hearts

Candy canes: (2)
Hot glue gun and glue stick
Trim: rick-rack

1. Place candy canes together creating heart shape. Using hot glue gun, adhere candy canes together.

2. Wrap rick-rack around top center of heart and tie in bow. Adhere in place.

Option: Ribbon may be used in place of rick-rack.

Snowflake

materials:

Glass beads: ⅛" round (8); ³⁄₁₆" round
(8); ¼" round (8); ⅝" round (1)
Needlenose pliers
Seed beads: 11/0 (8)
Wire: beading; medium gauge
Wire cutters

instructions:

1. Using wire cutters, cut four 3"
lengths of wire. Using needlenose pliers,
bend one end into loop. Thread seed
bead, ³⁄₁₆" bead, ¼" bead, two ⅛" beads,
¼" bead, ³⁄₁₆" bead, and seed bead on
wire. Bend end of wire into loop to
secure. Repeat with remaining wires.

2. Slide four beads to each looped end,
leaving middle of wire bare. Place one
beaded wire on top of another as shown
in Illustration A. Wire together with
beading wire. Repeat with two remaining
beaded wires. Place one set of beaded
wires on top of other as shown in
Illustration B. Wire together.

3. Thread length of beading wire
through ⅝" bead and wire to center of
beaded wires. Attach Snowflake to gift
with beading wire or fishing line.

Flower

materials:

Glass beads: ¼" round (20); ½" oval (10);
1" oval (20)
Needlenose pliers
Seed beads: 2/0 (1)
Wire: fine gauge
Wire cutters

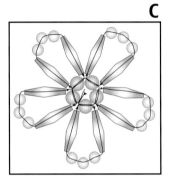

C

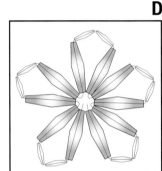

D

instructions:

1. Using wire cutters, cut 19" length of
wire. Thread 1" ovals and round beads on
wire as shown in Illustration C. Using
needlenose pliers, twist ends to secure.

2. Cut 17" length of wire. Thread ½" and
1" oval beads on wire as shown in
Illustration D, twisting wires together after
each loop. Twist ends to secure. Place wired
beads on top of wired beads from Step 1
and wire together.

3. Cut 4" length of wire. Thread 1" oval
and seed bead on wire. Bend wire in half
and thread back through oval bead. Twist
ends to secure. Place and center on top of
wired beads, wire to secure. Attach to gift
with beading wire or fishing line.

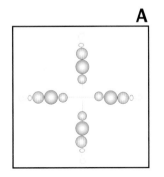

A

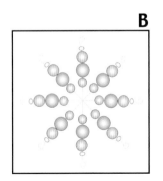

B

Star

materials:

Glass beads: ⅝" round (1); 1" oval (8)
Needlenose pliers
Seed beads: 11/0 (16)
Wire: beading; medium gauge
Wire cutters

instructions:

1. Using wire cutters, cut four 3" lengths of wire. Using needlenose pliers, bend one end into loop. Thread seed bead, two oval beads, and seed bead on wire. Bend end of wire into loop to secure. Repeat with remaining wires.

2. Slide three beads to each looped end, leaving middle of wire bare. Follow Steps 2 and 3 of Snowflake on opposite page. Attach Beaded to gift with beading wire or fishing line.

Tinsel Trim

materials:

Needlenose pliers
Pipe cleaners: chenille, metallic (1),
    metallic (2)
Wire cutters

instructions:

1. Bend chenille pipe cleaner as shown in photograph with ends going to the middle.

2. Bend metallic pipe cleaner as shown in photograph with ends going to the middle. Using needlenose pliers, pinch ends to a point.

3. Place pipe cleaner shape on top of chenille shape. Wrap remaining pipe cleaner around center of shapes and twist to secure. Bring one end of pipe cleaner to top of shapes and coil in center. Using wire cutters, cut off excess pipe cleaners.

Two-Hearts

materials:

Ribbon
Scissors: craft
Stamp pad: metallic gold (on example)
Wooden heart

instructions:

1. Using scissors, cut ribbon to desired length. Using wooden heart and stamp pad, stamp heart at each end of ribbon. Allow to dry. Trim around bottom of hearts.

Velvet Star

materials:

Bias tape or cording
Fabric: velvet
Pencil
Polyester stuffing
Scissors: craft, fabric
Sewing machine
Sewing needle
Straight pins
Thread
Tracing paper

instructions:

1. Using pencil and tracing paper, trace star pattern. *Option: Photocopy pattern to enlarge or reduce.* Using craft scissors, cut out pattern. Place and pin pattern to fabric. Using fabric scissors, cut out two stars. Cut length of bias tape for loop.

2. Fold bias tape in half. Pin to right side of fabric with loop to inside. Place and pin star fabric with right sides together. Using sewing machine, sew ¼" inseam around outside edge, leaving opening. Turn star right side out. Stuff star with polyester stuffing. Using sewing needle and thread, handstitch opening closed.

attach
bias tape

Star pattern
Cut 2

opening

Beaded Acorn

materials:

Acorn ornament
Beads
Copper wire: small gauge
Needlenose pliers
Wire cutters

instructions:

1. Using wire cutters, cut length of wire. Thread end of wire through ornament hanger. Using needlenose pliers, bend wire back and thread through first bead, twist to secure. Slide beads onto wire. Coil remaining wire to secure beads.

Boot Lace

materials:

Boot lace

instructions:

1. Place boot lace around box as desired and knot as shown in Illustration A.

A

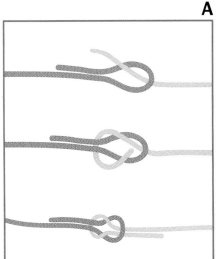

Naturally!

Fall leaves
Ribbon
Ting ting grass
Twine

1. Place leaf stems and ting ting grass together. Wrap with twine. Tie ribbon around bound stems.

Fishing

Acrylic paints
Craft knife
Découpage medium
Paintbrushes: (2)
Ribbon: ¼" metallic
Scissors: craft
Wooden fish: (3)
Wrapping paper

1. Using scissors, cut six pieces of wrapping paper slightly larger than fish. Using paintbrush, apply découpage to one side of fish. Adhere wrapping paper to fish. Allow to dry. Using craft knife, trim paper from edge of fish. Repeat for other side.

2. Using paintbrush, apply découpage over paper on fish. Allow to dry.

3. Paint sides of fish with paint to match wrapping paper. Allow to dry.

4. Thread ribbon through end of fish and tie loop. Slide loops onto ribbon and tie around gift.

Twig Knot

materials:

Cording
Scissors: craft
Twig

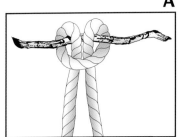

A

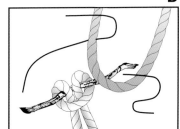

B

instructions:

1. Using scissors, cut cording long enough to wrap twice around gift lengthwise, plus 6".

2. Find center of cording and fold each end to the center. Place twig in the two folded ends as shown in Illustrations A–C. Center twig knot on gift and pull cord ends to backside of gift. Knot ends of cord to hold cord on gift. Cut off excess ends.

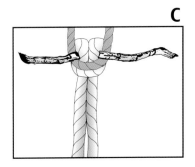

C

Copper Leaf

Metallic wrapped cord: fine,
    copper (our example)
Silk leaf: copper (our example)

1. Wrap length of cord around gift once. Curl leaf stem and wrap cord around leaf. Wrap cord one additional time and knot in back to secure.

Medallion

Craft glue
Medallion
Ribbon: ⅛"

1. Using craft glue, place glue to back-side center of medallion and adhere to top flap of wrap. Allow to dry.

2. Wrap one end of ribbon around edge of medallion. Wrap remaining end around gift and around edge of medallion to secure.

Nest Egg

Hot-glue gun and glue
    sticks
Nest
Polyester stuffing
Ribbon: 1½" wide,
    wire-edged hand-
    dyed silk or
    ombre (6")
Scissors: fabric

1. Using scissors, cut ribbon in half lengthwise to make eggs. Overlap raw edges and using hot-glue gun, adhere edges together forming tube. Gather one end of tube and adhere to secure. Stuff with stuffing. Gather remaining end and adhere to secure. Adhere eggs to nest with seam side down. Adhere nest to gift.

Daisies

materials:

Craft glue
Silk flowers
Styrofoam® block: circular, green
Wire cutters

instructions:

1. Using wire cutters, trim silk flower stem 2" from bloom. Apply small amount of glue on end of stem. Push stem into block. Repeat until block is covered with flowers. Adhere Daisies to gift.

Scarf Trim

materials:

Acrylic paint
Hot-glue and glue sticks
Paintbrush
Winter scarf
Wooden buttons: large (3)

instructions:

1. Using paintbrush, paint buttons as desired with acrylic paint. Tie scarf around wrapped package. Using hot-glue gun, adhere scarf to secure. Adhere buttons below scarf knot.

Note: Wrap gift in Sparkle on page 99 for snowman effect.

Delicate Bow

materials:

Paper clips (2)
Pipe cleaner
Scissors: craft
Tissue paper: 4 sheets

instructions:

1. Using craft scissors, cut 6" square sheets of tissue paper. Lay tissue papers on top of each other. Begin at long edge and fold tissue paper back and forth accordion-style.

2. Locate center of folded tissue strip and attach paper clip. Wrap pipe cleaner around paper clip once. Fold strip up in middle so ends meet.

3. Using fingers, separate some tissue layers. Attach second paper clip above first paper clip. Finish separating tissue and fluff.

Chenille Tree

materials:

Chenille pipe cleaner: green
Gold wire: fine-gauge
Hot-glue gun and glue sticks
Pipe cleaner: red
Toothpick
Wire cutters

instructions:

1. Bend chenille pipe cleaner in zigzag shape for tree. Twist small piece of pipe cleaner around top of tree.

2. Coil gold wire around toothpick. Slide wire off toothpick. Gently pull wire apart and coil around tree for garland. Using hot-glue gun, adhere Chenille Tree to gift.

Ribbon Rings

materials:

Hot-glue gun and glue sticks
Metal rings (3)
Ribbon

instructions:

1. Wrap ribbon around ring until covered. Using hot-glue gun, place a tiny dab of glue on ribbon ends to secure. Repeat for remaining rings.

2. Link two rings by wrapping ribbon around both rings. Adhere ribbon ends to back side. Repeat with remaining ring. Tie length of ribbon to each end ring.

Fabric Buds

materials:

Craft knife
Fabric
Hot-glue gun and glue sticks
Ribbon: wire-edged
Styrofoam® balls: small

instructions:

1. Using craft knife, trim off ball making one flat side.

2. Tear fabric into ⅜" strips. Using hot-glue gun, adhere one end of fabric strip to flat side of ball. Wrap fabric around ball to cover, adhering ends to flat side. Repeat with fabric strips until ball is covered.

3. Fold wire-edged ribbon into two loops and twist. Adhere flat side of ball between ribbon loops. *Option: Additional loops may be added.* Adhere Fabric Buds to gift.

Bow

Fabric: ¼ yd.
Iron and ironing board
Needle
Pipe cleaners: (2)
Scissors: fabric
Sewing machine
Thread

1. Using fabric scissors, cut two 16" x 9" rectangles from fabric. Place fabric with right sides together. Using sewing machine, sew ½" seam around outside edge of rectangles, leaving 2" unsewn in middle of long edge.

2. Using needle and thread, attach one pipe cleaner to each long side. Turn bow right side out. Using needle and thread, hand-stitch unsewn seam together.

3. Cut 4" x 3" rectangle. Fold each long side of fabric to center and using iron, press flat. Wrap around center of sewn rectangle, with raw edge to back of bow. Fold raw edge under and hand-stitch in place. Place gift ribbon over center of bow and tie to gift.

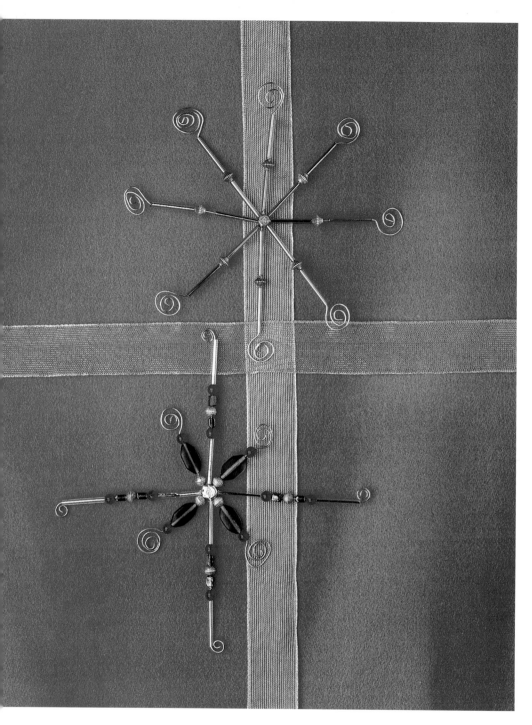

Bead Stars

materials:

Beads: assorted
    shapes and sizes
Flux
Needlenose pliers
Soldering iron and
    solder
Wire: 18-gauge
Wire cutters

instructions:

1. Using wire cutters, cut four equal lengths of wire. Place wires in Star shape as shown in photograph. Apply small amount of flux to center if wires and using soldering iron, solder wires together. Allow to cool.

2. Thread beads on wire as desired. Using pliers, shape end of wire as desired. Repeat with remaining wires.

materials:

Button: large
Chain: fine link
Spray paint: metallic
Wire: beading

instructions:

1. Using spray paint, spray button. Allow to dry. Sew button on center of chain with wire.

Paper Wire

materials:

Needlenose pliers
Paper wire
Ribbon (optional)

instructions:

1. Using needlenose pliers, shape wire as desired. *Option: Several wires can be grouped together and held in place by coiling wire around group.* Attach to gift with ribbon or cording.

Shape It

materials:

Curling ribbon (optional)
Pipe cleaners: metallic

instructions:

1. Shape pipe cleaners into spirals, stars, or other shapes. Connect pipe cleaners together by twisting around one another for more complex shapes. *Option: Tie on length of curling ribbon to attach to gift.*

Charmed

materials:

Beads: assorted (4)
Gem (1)
Hot-glue gun and glue sticks
Needlenose pliers (2)
Wire: 8-10 gauge, aluminum; beading, silver
Wire cutters

instructions:

1. Using wire cutters, cut 20" piece of aluminum wire. Locate center of wire and, using needle-nose pliers, bend wire in half. Hold top of bend with pliers and, using second pair of pliers, twist wires tightly together 4½" down. Bend untwisted ends as shown in photograph.

2. Cut 5" and 4" lengths of aluminum wire. Bend wires as shown in photograph. Attach smallest branch 1⅜" from top with beading wire. Attach remaining branch 1¾" below first branch. Thread beading wire through beads and attach one to each branch. Using hot-glue gun, adhere gem to top of tree. Attach to gift with beading wire or fishing line.

Twig Trim

materials:

Hot-glue gun and glue sticks
Jute
Pruners
Scissors: craft
Twigs (4)
Wildlife artwork

instructions:

1. Using scissors, cut artwork to desired size. Using pruners, cut two twigs 1" wider than width, and two twigs 1" longer than length of artwork.

2. Place twigs together to make frame. Using hot-glue gun, adhere sticks together. Wrap jute around each corner in criss-cross fashion, ending at back of frame. Adhere jute ends to secure.

3. Tie piece of jute around top of frame for loop. Adhere frame to front of artwork.

Corrugated

materials:

Card stock: corrugated
Eyelet punch and eyelets
Scissors: craft

instructions:

1. Using scissors, cut out desired shapes.

2. Using eyelet punch, place fastener in top of shape to secure.

6 *Wrapping Papers*

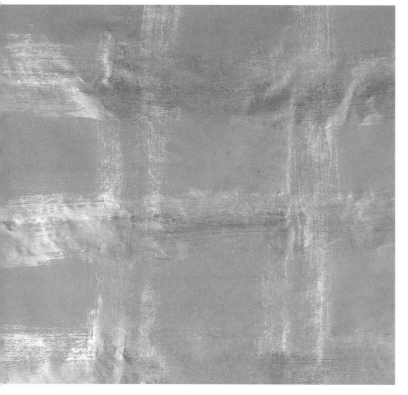

Silver & Gold

materials:

Acrylic paints: metallic gold; metallic silver (on example)
Kraft© paper
Paintbrush

instructions:

1. Using paintbrush, paint horizontal gold stripes on paper by dragging paintbrush across surface. Allow to dry. Repeat with vertical stripes.

2. Paint horizontal silver stripes next to horizontal gold stripes. Allow to dry. Repeat with vertical stripes. Allow to dry.

Tan Pastels

materials:

Chalk pastels
Fixative spray
Tissue paper

instructions:

1. Using pastels, decorate paper as desired. Spray surface of paper with fixative to keep pastels from smearing. Allow to dry.

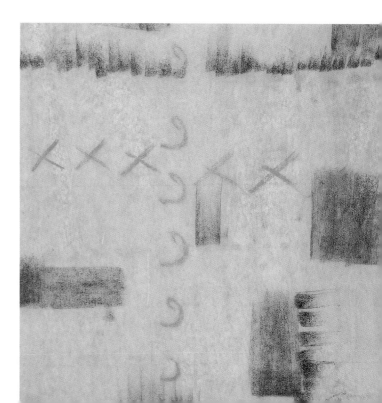

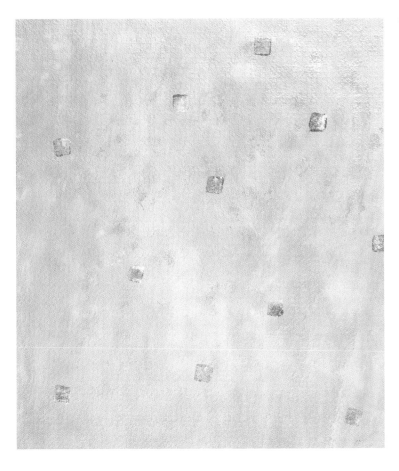

Wallpaper

materials:

Acrylic paints: metallic champagne; metallic gold; sand
Paintbrush: flat
Wallpaper

instructions:

1. Dilute sand and champagne paint to watercolor consistency. Using paintbrush, wash with sand on wrong side of wallpaper. Allow to dry. Apply wash with metallic champagne. Allow to dry.

2. Paint small squares randomly with gold paint. Allow to dry. Using tip of brush, paint small strokes of white on gold squares. Allow to dry.

Touch of Gold

materials:

Acrylic paints: metallic bronze; metallic lt. gold
Paintbrushes: flat, stiff; round
Wrapping paper: striped, gold

instructions:

1. Dilute paints to watercolor consistency. Using flat paintbrush, paint broad brush strokes randomly on paper with bronze paint. Allow to dry.

2. Using round paintbrush, paint small, short strokes as desired. Allow to dry.

Golden Threads

materials:

Webbing spray
Wrapping paper: striped

instructions:

1. Spray paper with webbing until desired effect is achieved. Allow to dry.

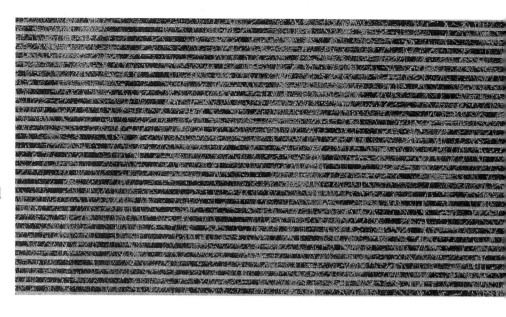

Celebrate

materials:

Acrylic paint: black;
   metallic silver
Butcher paper: black
Marker: fine line, white;
   medium, white
Paintbrush: flat

instructions:

1. Dilute black paint. Using paintbrush, paint broad strokes randomly on paper for textural effect. Allow to dry.

2. Using tip of paintbrush, dab silver paint sparingly. Allow to dry.

3. Using fine line marker, write words of choice. Using medium marker, write words of choice.

82

Oriental

materials:

Kraft© paper
Spray paints: black; red
(on example)

1. Lightly spray paper surface with black paint. Spray paper surface with short bursts of red paint until desired effect is achieved. Allow to dry.

Checkered Past

materials:

Marker
Newspaper
Pencil
Yardstick

instructions:

1. Using pencil and ruler, mark horizontal lines. Turn paper and mark vertical lines. *Note: Size of squares will require adjustment to fit size of giftbox.*

2. Using marker and starting in center of newspaper, color every other square. *Note: Select newspaper page that has some color or other design that will show between colored checks or applies to the recipient.*

Textured Tape

Acrylic paints: metallic copper;
    metallic gold; metallic purple;
    turquoise (on example)
Kraft© paper
Masking tape
Sea sponge
Sponge brush
Styrofoam® plates

instructions:

1. Apply vertical and horizontal rows of tape on paper. Tear small pieces of tape and place randomly on paper.

2. Using sea sponge, sponge turquoise paint to cover paper. Allow to dry. Lightly sponge with copper paint. Allow to dry.

3. Using sponge brush, streak purple paint randomly over taped areas. Streak gold metallic paint randomly over taped areas. Allow to dry.

Textured Color

materials:

Acrylic paints: charcoal; metallic copper;
    metallic gold; turquoise (on example)
Handmade paper: textured
Sea sponge

instructions:

1. Using sea sponge, sponge paper with turquoise paint. Allow to dry. Sponge with copper and gold paint randomly. Allow paint to dry between colors. Lightly sponge with charcoal. Allow to dry.

Stitched Stars

Mulberry paper
Pencil
Sea sponge
Sewing machine
Thread: two colors
Watercolor paint

1. Using pencil, mark stars and spirals on paper. Using sewing machine and thread, sew stars with one thread color and spirals with second color, following pencil marks.

2. Using sponge and watercolor paint, lightly sponge paint over sewn shapes. Allow to dry.

Crinkled Metallics

Finger-painting paper
Non-toxic powdered metallic pigments:
    copper; gold; turquoise (on example)
Spray water bottle

1. Using water spray bottle, spray paper surface. Lightly sprinkle metallic pigments over paper surface as desired. Spray paint with water. Scrunch paper into ball. Smooth paper out and allow to dry.

Spirals

materials:

Crayons
Spiral rubbing plate
Two-toned construction paper

instructions:

1. Place rubbing plate under paper. Using crayons, rub side of crayon over paper to create patterns. Move rubbing plate to new location and repeat until desired effect is achieved.

Map It Up

materials:

Map
Webbing spray

instructions:

1. Spread map out flat. Spray map with webbing spray until desired effect is achieved. Allow to dry.

Square Off

materials:

Kraft© paper
Paintbrush: flat
Pencil
Ruler
Sewing machine
Thread
Watercolor paints

instructions:

1. Using pencil and ruler, mark off horizontal lines. Mark off vertical lines. Using sewing machine, sew zigzag stitch over pencil marks.

2. Using paintbrush, paint squares randomly with watercolor wash. Allow to dry.

Stars & Plaids

materials:

Acrylic paint: metallic gold
Fixative spray
Kraft© paper
Liquid paint retarder
Pastels: green, red
Sponge star stamp

instructions:

1. Using side of green pastel, draw wide horizontal and vertical stripes on paper. Using tip of red pastel, draw narrow horizontal and vertical stripes on paper. Using spray fixative, spray paper surface. Allow to dry.

2. Mix paint with liquid paint retarder. Using star stamp, stamp stars over paper surface. Allow to dry.

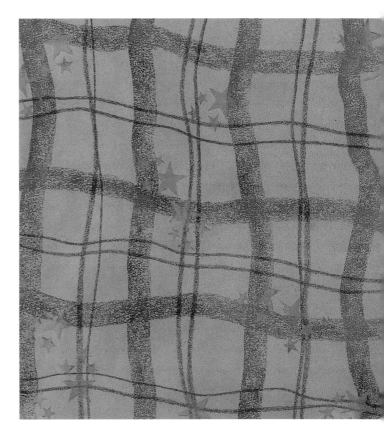

Finger Stars

materials:

Disposable bowl
Finger-painting paper
Liquid dishwashing soap
Measuring cup
Powdered tempera paint: yellow
Stir stick
Teaspoon measuring spoon
Water

instructions:

1. Pour ¼ cup tempera paint and 1 teaspoon liquid dishwashing soap into bowl. Using stir stick, add water and mix until paint is consistency of pudding.

2. Using hands, wet paper. Pour paint onto paper surface and smear, covering paper surface. Using finger, draw stars in paint. Allow to dry.

Rosy Pastels

materials:

Chalk pastels
Fixative spray
Tissue paper: red

instructions:

1. Using pastels, decorate paper as desired. Spray surface of tissue paper with fixative to keep pastels from smearing. Allow to dry.

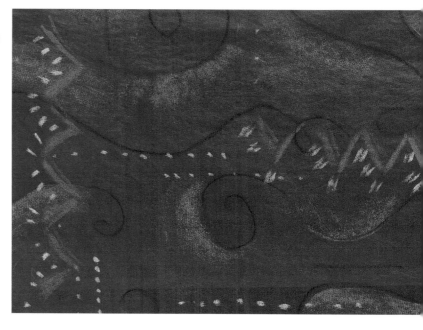

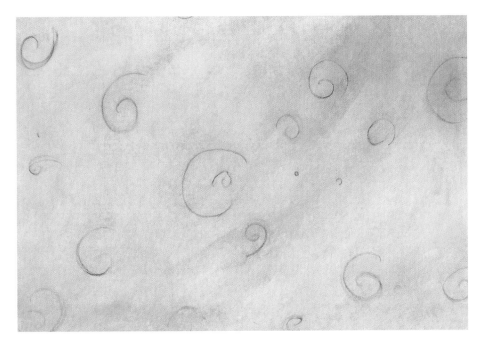

Pastels
materials:

materials:

Butcher paper
Chalk pastels
Fixative spray

instructions:

1. Using pastels, decorate paper as desired. Spray surface of paper with fixative to keep pastels from smearing. Allow to dry.

Ferns

materials:

Handmade paper: white
Paintbrush: large, round,
Sponge brush
Watercolor paints: burnt sienna;
    olive; turquoise; yellow-green

instructions:

1. Mix turquoise paint with water and using sponge brush, wash paint over paper. Allow to dry. Using round paintbrush, paint leaves with remaining colors. Allow colors to run into one another. Allow to dry.

Polka Dots

Acrylic paint
Butcher paper
Circle stencil
Sponge

instructions:

1. Using circle stencil and sponge, sponge circles on paper with paint as desired. Allow to dry.

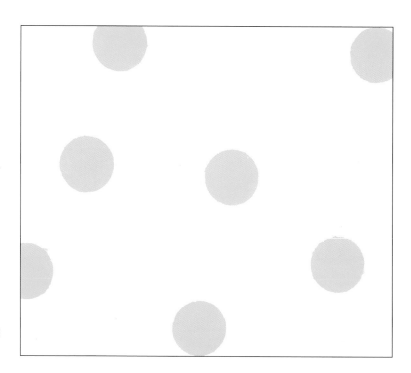

Paper Stars

materials:

Construction Paper
Pencil
Scissors: craft
Star stencil: varying sizes

instructions:

1. Using star stencil and pencil, trace stars on paper. Using scissors, cut out stars. Laminate stars in random pattern to create sheet of wrapping paper.

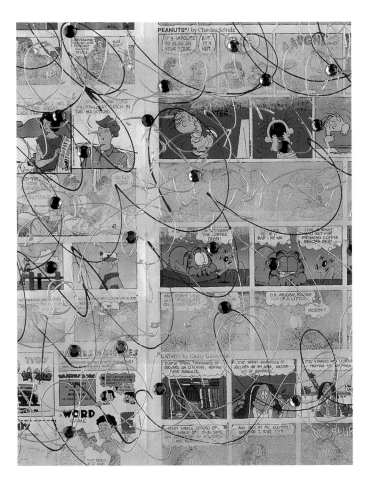

Funky Comics

materials:

Acrylic paint
Acrylic tube paints: 2 colors
Colored comic strips
Craft glue (optional)
Rhinestones
Roller brush or brayer

instructions:

1. Using roller brush, roll on vertical stripes with acrylic paint. Allow to dry.

2. Paint squiggly lines over surface of paper with acrylic tube paints as desired.

3. Attach rhinestones to wet paint as desired. Allow to dry. *Option: Craft glue may be used to attach rhinestones.*

Picture This

materials:

Photograph

instructions:

1. Color copy photograph to desired dimensions.

Kiss Flowers

materials:

Acrylic paints: pink; purple; turquoise; yellow (on example)
Candy kisses (4)
Cellophane: clear
Scissors: craft
Styrofoam® plate

instructions:

1. Pour small amount of each acrylic paint onto plate. Using wrapped candy kiss, dip bottom of kiss into paint and stamp onto cellophane to make flower design. Repeat until cellophane is covered with flowers. Allow to dry.

Scrunched

materials:

Plastic wrap
Powdered tempera paint: magenta; purple; turquoise (on example)
Rubber bands (3)
Spray water bottle
Straight pin

instructions:

1. Remove lids from tempera paints. Using plastic wrap and rubber bands, cover paint bottle openings. Using straight pin, poke holes in plastic wrap.

2. Using water bottle, spray paper surface. Sprinkle paint colors randomly over paper surface. Spray paper with water. Scrunch paper into ball. Smooth paper out and allow to dry.

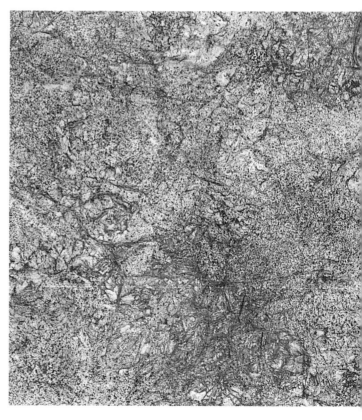

Pastel Hearts

Butcher paper: white
Card stock
Chalk pastels
Facial tissue
Pencil
Scissors: craft
Spray fixative

1. Using pastels, lightly color entire paper with two to three pastel colors. Using facial tissue, blend pastel colors together.

2. Using pencil, draw four hearts of varying sizes on card stock. Using craft scissors, cut out hearts. Color center of hearts with two to three different colors.

3. Place hearts, pastel side up, on paper as desired. Using facial tissue, smudge color from center of heart outward on all sides, creating a reverse heart outline. Hearts may be reused as often as desired. Using spray fixative, spray finished paper surface. Allow to dry.

Chalkboard

Butcher paper: black
Colored chalks
Spray fixative

1. Using chalk, write alphabet letters randomly. Spray surface of paper with fixative to keep chalk from smearing. Allow to dry.

93

Forest

Disposable bowls (2)
Finger-painting paper
Liquid dishwashing soap
Measuring cup
Powdered tempera paint: blue; yellow
Stir sticks (2)
Teaspoon measuring spoon

instructions:

1. Pour 2 tablespoons each of yellow and green paint, and 1 teaspoon liquid dishwashing soap into bowl. Using stir stick, add water a little at a time, and mix until consistency of pudding. Place ⅓ of paint into second bowl and add yellow paint to make yellow-green. Add water as needed.

2. Using hands, wet paper. Pour colors onto paper surface and smear together, covering surface. Using finger, draw trees in paint. Allow to dry.

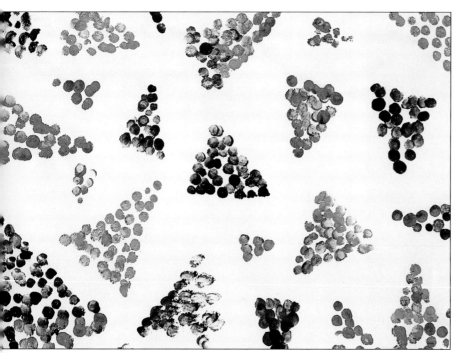

Trees

materials:

See above Forest materials list.

instructions:

1. Refer to above Forest Step #1.

2. Dip fingertips into paints and press on paper to create design. Allow to dry.

Petroglyphs

materials:

Chalk pastels
Spray fixative
Tissue paper

instructions:

1. Using pastels, decorate paper as desired. Spray surface of tissue paper with fixative to keep pastels from smearing. Allow to dry.

Spattered

materials:

Acrylic paints: lime green;
    mauve; turquoise;
    yellow (on example)
Kraft© paper
Paintbrush

instructions:

1. Dilute paint with water. Using paintbrush, splatter paint, one color at a time, over paper until desired effect is achieved. Allow to dry.

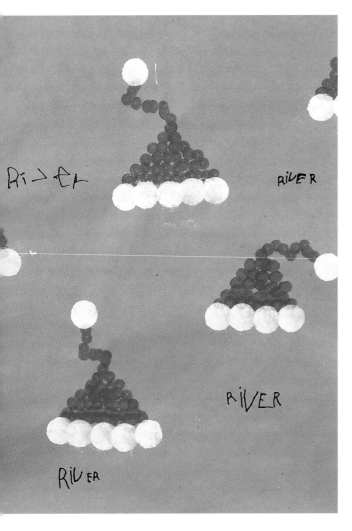

Santa's Hat

materials:

Acrylic paint: white
Circle stencil
Glitter dust: white
Kraft© paper
Marker: medium point, black
Paintbrush
Paint-dot marker: red
Pencil

instructions:

1. Using paint-dot marker, place dots in shape of Santa's hat. Allow to dry.

2. Using pencil and stencil, draw circles for fur trim and tip of hat. Using paintbrush, paint circles with acrylic paint. Sprinkle circles with glitter dust. Allow to dry.

3. Using marker, write name of recipient or giver on paper.

Folk Art

materials:

Fabric
Glitter spray
Glue stick
Kraft© paper
Scissors: fabric

instructions:

1. Using fabric scissors, cut out fabric designs. Using glue stick, apply glue to wrong side of fabric. Adhere on paper as desired. Using glitter spray, spray paper. Allow to dry.

Snowmen

materials:

Acrylic paint: white
Circle stencils: varying sizes
Glitter powder: white
Kraft© paper
Paintbrush
Pencil
Tube paint: black

instructions:

1. Using pencil and circle stencils, draw snowman on paper. Using paintbrush, paint snowman with white paint. Sprinkle glitter powder on wet paint and allow to dry. Repeat for each snowman.

2. Using tube paint, draw arms, buttons, face, hat, and scarf.

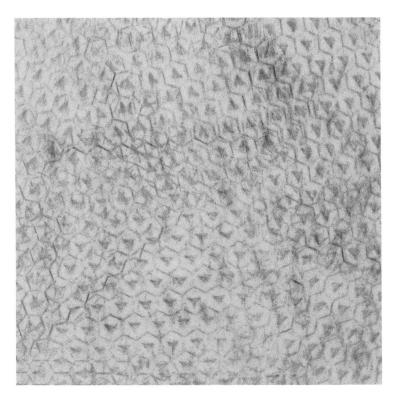

Honeycomb

materials:

Crayons
Rubbing plate
Two-toned construction paper

instructions:

1. Place rubbing plate under paper. Using crayons, rub side of crayons over paper to create patterns. Move rubbing plate to new location and repeat until desired effect is achieved. *Option: Any textured surface may be used as a rubbing plate.*

Star Bright

materials:

Adhesive spray
Construction paper
Craft knife
Glitter: silver
Pencil
Star cookie cutter
Tissue paper: silver

instructions:

1. Using pencil, trace around cookie cutter on construction paper to make shield. Using craft knife, cut out star. Discard star.

2. Place shield and cookie cutter on tissue paper. Using spray adhesive, spray inside cookie cutter on tissue paper. Sprinkle paper surface inside cookie cutter with glitter. Remove shield and cookie cutter. Continue to place shield and cookie cutter to repeat design until desired effect is achieved.

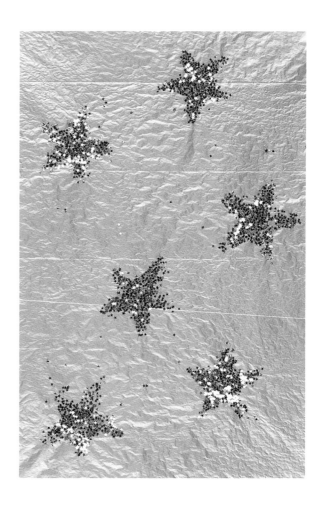

Silver Stars

materials:

Acrylic paint: metallic silver
Paintbrush
Star stamp
Wrapping paper: metallic silver

instructions:

1. Using paintbrush, paint star stamp and stamp stars on paper randomly. Allow to dry.

Silver Lining

materials:

Butcher paper: blue
Metallic paint: silver
Waxed paper

instructions:

1. Pour metallic paint onto waxed paper and smear paint. Fold waxed paper in half and press paint around. Open waxed paper with paint side up. Place butcher paper on waxed paper and rub butcher paper to print. Remove paper from waxed paper and allow to dry.

2. Add additional paint to waxed paper and repeat above until desired effect is achieved. Waxed paper may be used three to four times before being replaced.

Sparkle

materials:

Butcher paper
Glitter: clear
Glitter powder: clear; white
Spray adhesive

instructions:

1. Using spray adhesive, spray paper surface until covered. Sprinkle paper surface with glitter powders. Allow to dry. *Note: Do large sheets of paper in sections.*

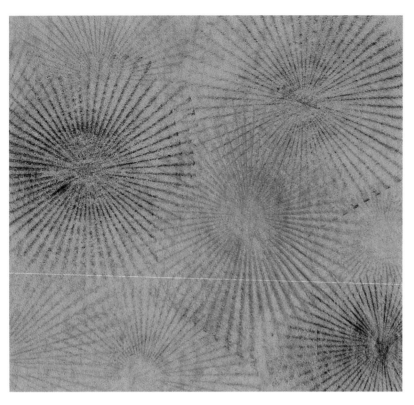

Starburst

materials:

Crayons
Rubbing plate
Two-toned construction paper

instructions:

1. Place rubbing plate under paper. Using crayons, rub side of crayons over paper to create patterns. Move rubbing plate to new location and repeat until desired effect is achieved. *Option: Any textured surface may be used as a rubbing plate.*

Sprinkled

materials:

Finger painting paper
Plastic wrap
Powdered tempera paints: blue; magenta; turquoise; yellow (on example)
Rubber bands (4)
Straight pin
Spray water bottle

instructions:

1. Remove tempera paint lid. Cover with plastic wrap. Place rubber band over plastic wrap to secure. Using pin, poke holes in plastic wrap.

2. Spray paper with water. Sprinkle powdered paints over surface randomly. Lightly mist paint and allow to dry.

Frosted

materials:

Finger-painting paper
Plastic wrap
Powdered tempera paint: blue; magenta;
    purple; yellow (on example)
Rubber bands (4)
Spray water bottle
Straight pin

instructions:

1. Refer to Sprinkled Step #1 on opposite page.

2. Using water bottle, spray paper surface. Sprinkle paint colors randomly over paper surface as desired. Spray paint with water. Using plastic wrap, cover paint and paper. Pat plastic wrap down on paint with hands. Allow to dry and remove plastic wrap.

Frosted Too

materials:

Plastic wrap
Powdered tempera paint: blue; magenta;
    red; yellow (on example)
Rubber bands (4)
Spray water bottle
Straight pin

instructions:

1. Refer to Sprinkled Step #1 on opposite page.

2. Using water bottle, spray paper surface. Sprinkle paint colors randomly over paper surface as desired. Spray paper with water. Scrunch up piece of plastic wrap. Dab up and down on wet paint surface until desired effect is achieved. Allow to dry.

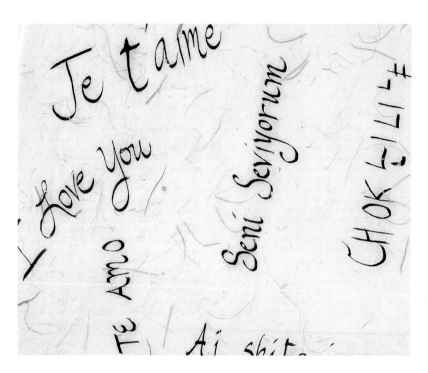

I Love You

I Love You

materials:

Calligraphy pen
Mulberry paper

instructions:

1. Using calligraphy pen, write "I love you" in different languages randomly on paper.

Antiqued

materials:

3-d sculpture medium
Antique découpage medium
Butcher paper: white
Disposable soft cloth
Old paintbrush
Opaque paint marker: metallic gold
Paste shoe polish: brown

instructions:

1. Using hands, smear sculpture medium over paper surface. Allow to dry.

2.. Using paintbrush, apply antique découpage medium to paper. Allow to dry.

3. Using soft cloth, wipe paper surface with transparent layer of shoe polish. Allow to dry. Using metallic markers, write desired words randomly on paper.

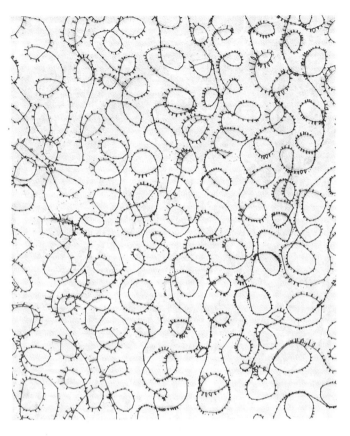

Stitched

materials:

Pencil
Rice paper
Sewing machine
Sponge
Thread: 2 colors
Watercolor paint

instructions:

1. Using pencil, mark desired shapes on paper. Using sewing machine and thread, stitch, following pencil marks.

2. Using sponge and watercolor paint, lightly sponge paint over stitched shapes.

Book Wrap

materials:

Craft knife
Discarded book
Metal-edged ruler

instructions:

1. Select desired page or pages from book. Using craft knife and metal-edged ruler, cut page from book. *Note: If gift is larger than book page, try enlarging by making photocopy.*

Chapter 6

"Let's name things I like, things I don't like," Libby said when I came into her room in the morning. Though she went to sleep with hardly a fuss, she liked my attention in the mornings, needing to ease herself into the day. It was going to be difficult to go back to work in September and give up these lazy times. We'd have to get into a schedule if we were all going to be out by eight o'clock.

"Let's see," I said, pulling back the yellow sheets and getting in next to her. She was still warm with sleep and delicious. I cupped her little behind in my hand. "You like Cheerios for breakfast, and I have some."

"I like Honey Nut better than plain, though," she noted.

"Yes. Next time we go to the store we'll buy Honey Nut Cheerios."

"What else do I like?" Libby turned around and nuzzled my neck, staring up at me. Her eyes were coffee-colored, like Jesse's, and they had a sensual droop that sometimes gave her face a wise, knowing look.

"You like Becky Jorganson and Teri and Amanda," I said.

"And Shannon Groovner," Libby added.

"Who's Shannon Groovner?"

"A boy who used to hit, but now he's nice."

Pearlescent

materials:

Découpage medium
Handmade paper: dk. green (on example)
Paintbrush
Pearlescent spray paint: green; pink; purple (on example)
Seed beads: varying sizes and colors
Spray bottle

instructions:

1. Using spray paint, spray paper randomly with each color. Allow to dry. Wrinkle paper and flatten. Spray paper with each color again. Allow to dry.

2. Mix découpage medium with water to thin consistency. Apply medium to paper randomly. Sprinkle beads onto découpage medium. Allow to dry.

Fall Leaves

materials:

Acrylic paints: browns; oranges; reds
Construction paper: orange
Découpage medium: matte
Embroidery floss: brown variegated
Liquid paint retarder
Paintbrush: large
Sponge stamps: leaf, varying sizes
Watercolor paint: browns; oranges; reds

instructions:

1. Using paintbrush, paint paper surface with wash combination of all watercolor paint colors. Allow to dry.

2. Mix acrylic paints with liquid paint retarder. Using paintbrush, paint leaf stamps with combination of all colors. Stamp leaves on paper as desired. Allow to dry.

3. Using découpage medium, attach length of sewing floss to paper as desired. Allow to dry.

7 *Wrap It Up*

Combine wraps, bows, trims, and tags to create beautiful and unique giftwrap.

Wrap a gift in Ferns on page 89 and trim with Wire Hearts on page 58.

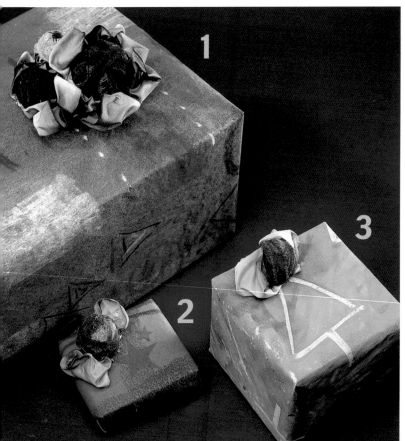

Trim a gift with Fabric Buds on page 74 and wrap in:

1. Petroglyphs on page 95.

2. Stars & Plaids on page 87.

3. Forest on page 94.

Trim a gift with Ribbon Rings on page 74 and wrap in:

1. Purchased glossy wrap that has been crumpled and smoothed out.

2. Stitched Stars on page 85.

3. Silver Stars on page 98.

1. Wrap a gift in Chalkboard on page 93 and trim with thin strips of corrugated paper.

2. Wrap a gift in Spattered on page 95 and trim with sheer ribbon.

Trim a gift with a Net Bow on page 56
and wrap in:

1. Wallpaper on page 81.

2. I Love You on page 102.

3. Tan Pastels on page 80.

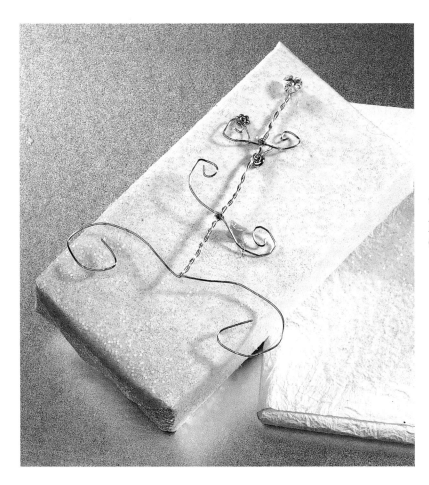

Wrap a gift in Sparkle on page 99 and trim with Charmed on page 78.

Wrap a gift in Picture This on page 91 using black-and-white photos. Trim with antique-style ribbon bows or trim.

Wrap a gift in Picture This on page 91 and trim with:

1. Cheesecloth and ribbon to create a mummy wrap.

2. Two Boot Lace ties on page 68.

1. Wrap a gift in Book Wrap on page 103. Trim with an old pair of eyeglasses and ribbon bow.

2. Trim a gift with a Silverware tag on page 51 and sheer ribbon. Wrap in culinary wrapping paper.

1. Wrap a gift in Square Off on page 87 and trim with Rusty Angel on page 60.

2. Wrap a gift in Honeycomb on page 97 and trim with Rusty Stars on page 61.

3. Wrap a gift in Silver & Gold on page 80 and trim with Tin Angel on page 61.

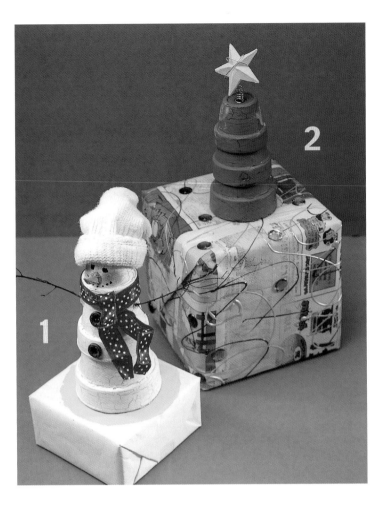

1. Wrap a gift in Polka Dots on page 90 and trim with Snowman Topper on page 62.

2. Wrap a gift in Funky Comics on page 91 and trim with Tree Topper on page 62.

1. Wrap a gift in Rosy Pastels on page 88 and trim with Chenille Tree on page 73.

Trim a gift with Paper Wire on page 77 and wrap in:

1. Pastels wrap on page 89.

2. Two-tone construction paper.

1. Wrap a gift in Snowmen on page 97 and trim with Rick-Rack Hearts on page 63 and wire-edged ribbon bow. *Option: Use red candy canes and embellish with holiday decorations.*

2. Wrap a gift in Santa's Hat on page 96 and trim with Rick-Rack Hearts on page 63 and a sheer ribbon bow.

3. *Options: Create a Christmas Tree wrap using the paint method for Santa's Hat on page 96.*

Trim a gift with 3d Hearts on page 59 and sheer ribbon, and wrap in:

1. Crinkled Metallics on page 85.

2. Kraft© paper

3. Scrunched on page 92.

1. Wrap a gift in Silver Lining on page 99. Trim with Snowflake on page 64 and fine metallic cording.

2. Wrap a gift in Star Bright on page 98. Trim with Flower on page 64 and fine metallic cording.

Boxes & Containers 8

2. Using scissors, cut vellum into square large enough for corners to pull up diagonally and overlap slightly. Place box on vellum and cut on dashed lines as shown in Illustration A. Fold up ends of vellum and overlap on top of box. Secure with tape. Fold up sides of vellum and overlap on top of box. Secure with tape. Secure star in center of box with tape.

Vellum Cover

materials:

Decorative box
Double-sided tape
Heat gun
Scissors: craft
Sealing wax: gold
Vellum
Wooden star

instructions:

1. Place piece of sealing wax on top of star. Using heat gun, heat sealing wax until it melts and runs down sides of star. Set aside to cool.

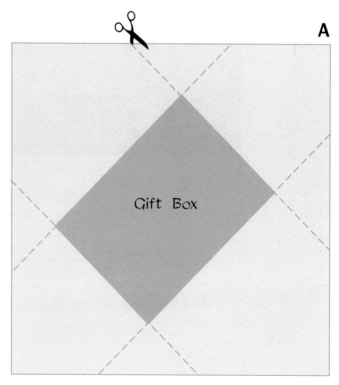

A

Gift Box

Découpage Clay Pots

Découpage medium
Glitter powder: clear
Glitter spray: gold
Paintbrush
Ribbon (optional)
Terra cotta pot
Tissue paper or napkins:
    decorative

1. Using paintbrush, apply découpage medium to bottom section of pot. Adhere tissue paper to pot. Allow to dry. Apply découpage medium over tissue paper. Sprinkle glitter powder on tissue. Allow to dry.

2. Using glitter spray, spray outside of pot to cover. Allow to dry. *Option: Place ribbon around pot and tie in bow.* Place gifts in pot.

Glitter Photo

materials:

Adhesive spray
Cording or ribbon
Foil gift box
Glitter spray: gold
Photograph

1. Color copy photograph, enlarging to desired dimensions. Spray back of color copy with adhesive. Center and place color copy on box lid; smooth flat.

2. Spray photograph with glitter. Allow to dry. Place gift in box and tie with cording or ribbon.

Découpage Photo

materials:

Decorative gift box
Découpage medium
Paintbrush
Photograph
Ribbon: sheer

1. Color copy photograph, enlarging to desired dimensions. Using paintbrush, apply découpage medium on back of color copy. Center and place color copy on box lid; smooth flat. Allow to dry. Apply décou-page medium over box lid. Allow to dry. Place gift in box and tie with ribbon.

Gift Glass

materials:

Acrylic paints
    (optional)
Candle: votive
Candleholder:
    votive (to fit
    jar top)
Canning jar
Canning ring
Paintbrush
    (optional)
Ribbon:
    wire-edged
Spray paints:
    gloss; metallic
Spray sealer: gloss

instructions:

1. Spray outside of jar with gloss paint until opaque.
Allow to dry. Spray outside of jar with metallic paint
until gloss paint is completely covered. Allow to dry.
*Option: Using paintbrush, paint design on outside of
jar. Allow to dry. Spray painted design with sealer.
Allow to dry.*

2. Place gift inside of jar. Place candleholder
in mouth of jar. Screw canning ring on jar to secure
candleholder in place. Tie ribbon around canning ring.
Place candle in candleholder.

Frosted Glass

Acrylic paint
Glass ornament
Jar
Ribbon
Spray Frost

1. Spray jar twice with frost, allowing jar to dry between coats.

2. Dip glass ornament into acrylic paint. Allow to dry. Place gift inside jar. Tie ribbon around mouth of jar and place ornament on top.

Foil Finish

materials:

Box: cylinder (on example)
Cording
Craft glue
Drawer pull
Hammer and large nail
Paintbrush: flat
Ribbon: moiré
Scissors: craft; fabric
Screwdriver
Spray paint: metallic
Tassel: small with loop
Wrapping paper: foil

instructions:

1. Using craft scissors, cut wrapping paper 1" wider than circumference of cylinder and 1" longer than height. Using paintbrush, apply thin layer of glue to outside of cylinder and adhere paper. Apply glue to inside top of cylinder. Fold paper to inside to adhere. Apply glue to bottom outside edge of cylinder. Fold paper around bottom of cylinder and adhere. Using bottom of cylinder for pattern, cut piece from wrapping paper. Adhere wrapping paper to bottom of cylinder. Allow to dry.

2. Cut wrapping paper 1" wider than circumference of lid and 1" longer than height. Adhere paper to side of lid, following instructions in Step 1. Using top of lid for pattern, cut piece from wrapping paper. Adhere wrapping paper to top of lid. Allow to dry.

3. Using fabric scissors, cut ribbon 1" longer than circumference of lid. Adhere ribbon to side of lid, folding under side ½".

4. Spray drawer pull with metallic paint. Allow to dry. Using hammer and nail, punch hole in top of lid. Using screwdriver, attach drawer pull to top of lid to secure.

5. Punch one hole on each side of cylinder. Thread tassel loop onto cording. Thread cording ends through holes and knot on the inside.

Velvet Touch

materials:

Box: cylinder (on example)
Cording
Fabric: velvet
Hammer and nail
Hot-glue gun and glue sticks
Ruler
Scissors: fabric
Spray paint
Tassel
Wooden bead: large

instructions:

1. Using scissors, cut fabric ½" wider than circumference of cylinder and ½" longer than height, excluding area that lid covers. Using hot-glue gun, apply strip of glue down side of cylinder. Adhere long edge of fabric to cylinder, folding under bottom and top raw edges ¼". Allow to cool. Apply strip of glue around top and bottom of cylinder. Stretch fabric tightly around cylinder, folding under bottom and top edges ¼". Fold under raw edge and adhere.

2. Using top of lid for pattern, cut fabric ¼" wider than circumference. Adhere fabric onto top of lid, stretching tight and pulling fabric down over edge. Cut fabric ½" longer than circumference and same width as height of lid. Adhere fabric to side of lid. Allow to cool. Wrap and adhere fabric onto side of lid, folding raw edges under.

3. Fold cording in half and adhere tassel to folded end. Spray bead with paint. Allow to dry. Thread bead onto cording. Using hammer and nail, punch hole in top center of lid. Thread raw ends of cording through hole on lid and knot on the inside.

Stamped

materials:

Box
Leaf stamp
Paintbrush
Stamp pad: black
Watercolor paint: green

instructions:

1. Using paintbrush, paint leaf shapes similar to leaf stamp with watercolor.

2. Using leaf stamp and stamp pad, stamp leaves over watercolor leaves.

Star Box

materials:

Adhesive spray
Cinnamon sticks
Corrugated paper
Découpage medium
Handmade paper
Hemp string
Hot-glue gun and
    glue sticks
Papier-mâché box with lid
Rusty tin stars: large (1);
    small (2)
Scissors: craft

instructions:

1. Using craft scissors, cut handmade paper to fit outside of box and edge of lid with ¼" overlap. Using adhesive spray, spray one side of box at a time. Adhere paper to box. Allow to dry. Repeat with lid. Allow to dry.

2. Cut strip of corrugated paper to fit outside of box. Apply découpage to back of paper. Adhere to box as shown in photograph.

3. Using hot-glue gun, glue cinnamon sticks to top of lid.

4. Wrap string around corrugated paper and thread through holes in large star and tie. Using hot-glue gun, adhere star to box. Adhere or tie small stars to end of string.

Flower Boxes

For one Box

materials:

Adhesive spray
Artificial flower: paper or silk
Braid
Empty round oatmeal box with lid
Hot-glue and glue sticks
Scissors: craft
Wrapping paper

instructions:

1. Using scissors, cut paper, following Foil Finish Steps 1 and 2 on page 120. Spray outside of oatmeal box with adhesive. Gently press and smooth wrapping paper around outside of box. Spray bottom of box with adhesive, fold under excess paper and press to adhere. Spray lid with adhesive and, following Step 2 on page 120, adhere paper to lid.

2. Using hot-glue gun, adhere braid to box as desired. Adhere flower to top of lid.

Tree Box

materials:

Adhesive spray
Cinnamon sticks (2)
Handmade paper: gold; green; red
Hot-glue gun and glue sticks
Papier-mâché box with lid
Scissors: craft

instructions:

1. Refer to Star Box Step 1. Using craft scissors, cut green paper to fit top of lid. Adhere paper to lid.

2. Tear triangle from green paper for tree, and adhere to box. Tear star from gold paper, and adhere to box.

3. Using hot-glue gun, adhere cinnamon sticks to base of tree for trunk.

Fancy

materials:

Box with lid
Scissors: craft
Spray adhesive
Wrapping paper

instructions:

1. Using craft scissors, cut paper to size for shoe box and lid. Using spray adhesive, spray bottom and sides of box.

2. Lay wrapping paper flat with design side down. Place bottom of box centered on wrapping paper. Place hands inside box and press down adhering box to wrapping paper. Smooth wrapping paper up sides of box, pressing so paper adheres to box. Complete the wrapping by folding ends of box in like traditional gift wrap, using additional spray adhesive as necessary to secure ends.

3. Repeat steps 1 and 2 for box lid.

Gift Hat

materials:

Hot-glue gun and
glue sticks
Metallic ribbon
Mylar® cellophane:
metallic colors
Party hat: metallic

instructions:

1. Place gift inside cellophane paper and tie closed with metallic ribbon.

2. Using hot-glue gun, glue party hat to cellophane.

Paint Can

materials:

Acrylic paint
New paint can

instructions:

1. Drizzle acrylic paint around rim of can, allowing paint to run down the sides. Allow to dry.

Option: Make a Paintbrush tag for trim.

Tissue Cans

materials:

Découpage medium
Drill and drill bit
Easter grass
Empty can
Hot-glue gun and glue sticks
Paintbrush
Ribbon
Tissue paper
Trim

instructions:

1. Using paintbrush, apply découpage medium to outside of can. Place tissue paper on découpage medium around outside of can. Allow to dry.

2. Using hot-glue gun, adhere trim to outside of can as desired.

3. Using drill and drill bit, drill hole on each side of can. Place ribbon through holes and tie for handle. Fill with Easter grass.

Barbed Wire Bucket

Needlenose pliers
Rusty Bucket
Weathered wire

1. Using needlenose pliers, remove original bucket handle. Attach barbed wire for handle to bucket and twist to secure.

Note: Spray a new bucket with rust spray or paint.

Note: Interior will need to be covered if filling bucket with candy.

Rusty Bucket

Needlenose pliers
Rusty bucket
Rusty tin elk (on example)
Rusty wire: medium-weight

1. Using needlenose pliers, place wire through holes in tin elk and attach wire to bucket handle, twisting wire to secure.

Chained Rusty Bucket

Needlenose pliers
Rusty bucket
Rusty chain
Rusty wire: medium-weight

1. Using needlenose pliers, remove original bucket handle.

2. Place small length of wire through handle hole and slide chain over wire. Twist wire to secure chain.

Index

Metric Equivalency Chart

mm–millimetres   cm–centimetres
inches to millimetres and centimetres

inches	mm	cm	inches	cm	inches	cm
1/8	3	0.3	9	22.9	30	76.2
1/4	6	0.6	10	25.4	31	78.7
3/8	10	1.0	11	27.9	32	81.3
1/2	13	1.3	12	30.5	33	83.8
5/8	16	1.6	13	33.0	34	86.4
3/4	19	1.9	14	35.6	35	88.9
7/8	22	2.2	15	38.1	36	91.4
1	25	2.5	16	40.6	37	94.0
1 1/4	32	3.2	17	43.2	38	96.5
1 1/2	38	3.8	18	45.7	39	99.1
1 3/4	44	4.4	19	48.3	40	101.6
2	51	5.1	20	50.8	41	104.1
2 1/2	64	6.4	21	53.3	42	106.7
3	76	7.6	22	55.9	43	109.2
3 1/2	89	8.9	23	58.4	44	111.8
4	102	10.2	24	61.0	45	114.3
4 1/2	114	11.4	25	63.5	46	116.8
5	127	12.7	26	66.0	47	119.4
6	152	15.2	27	68.6	48	121.9
7	178	17.8	28	71.1	49	124.5
8	203	20.3	29	73.7	50	127.0

Diane
Fitzgerald's
FAVORITE BEADING PROJECTS

Designs from Stringing to Beadweaving

Diane Fitzgerald's
FAVORITE BEADING PROJECTS

LARK CRAFTS
Asheville

To all my students
far and wide. I hope
your beading brings
you pleasure.

Editor
Nathalie Mornu

Technical Editor
Bonnie Brooks

Editorial Assistants
Abby Haffelt,
Dawn Dillingham

Editorial Intern
Virginia M. Roper

Art Director
Kathleen Holmes

Book and Cover Designer
Pamela Norman

Junior Designer
Carol Morse Barnao

Art Intern
Melissa Morrisey

Photographer
Lynne Harty

Illustrator
J'aime Allene

LARK CRAFTS

An Imprint of Sterling Publishing
387 Park Avenue South
New York, NY 10016

If you have questions or comments about
this book, please visit: larkcrafts.com

Library of Congress Cataloging-in-Publication Data

Fitzgerald, Diane.
  Diane Fitzgerald's favorite beading projects : designs from stringing to beadweaving / Diane Fitzgerald. -- 1st ed.
    p. cm.
  Includes index.
  ISBN 978-1-60059-922-4 (hc-plc : alk. paper)
  1. Beadwork. I. Title.
  TT860.F573 2012
  746.5--dc23
                              2011022951

10 9 8 7 6 5 4 3 2 1

First Edition

Published by Lark Crafts
An Imprint of Sterling Publishing Co., Inc.
387 Park Avenue South, New York, NY 10016

Text © 2012, Diane Fitzgerald
Photography © 2012, Lark Crafts, an Imprint of Sterling Publishing Co., Inc., unless otherwise specified
Photos on pages 22-24 and 123 © Diane Fitzgerald
Illustrations © 2012, Lark Crafts, an Imprint of Sterling Publishing Co., Inc., unless otherwise specified

Distributed in Canada by Sterling Publishing,
c/o Canadian Manda Group, 165 Dufferin Street
Toronto, Ontario, Canada M6K 3H6

Distributed in the United Kingdom by GMC Distribution Services,
Castle Place, 166 High Street, Lewes, East Sussex, England BN7 1XU

Distributed in Australia by Capricorn Link (Australia) Pty Ltd.,
P.O. Box 704, Windsor, NSW 2756 Australia

ISBN 13: 978-1-60059-922-4

For information about custom editions, special sales, and premium and corporate purchases, please contact the Sterling Special Sales Department at 800-805-5489 or specialsales@sterlingpub.com.

Submit requests for information about desk and examination copies available to college and university professors to academic@larkbooks.com. Our complete policy can be found at www.larkcrafts.com.

Contents

Introduction

Dear Reader,

When my beadwork odyssey began some 20 years ago, I couldn't have predicted it would last so long or introduce me to so many wonderful people. It has been a journey like no other.

The inspiration for my designs comes from many sources: historical beadwork, classes in color theory, contemporary and vintage jewelry, travel, nature, and geometry. (While I'm not a math wizard, I'm not put off by it, and I value and use the math I learned in high school.) Computers have helped, too, both to search for design ideas and to document and share my ideas and discoveries.

This book presents two dozen projects I've taught over the years, ranging from beginner to intermediate level, plus a gallery of other pieces to inspire you. It's hard to say which of these is my favorite. Each one elicits special memories, among them:

● teaching the One-to-Many Strand Necklace at the Second International Bead Conference;

● donating the Zipper Bracelet pattern to the Worcestershire Beaders to make as a charity fund raising project;

● giving the whimsical Button Doll to family members at Christmas;

● and wearing the Merry Cherries Necklace to my grandson's wedding.

When I look back on my career, what comes to mind the most is how much I've learned from students, and also the pleasure my students have found in working on and completing a piece. Many of my fondest memories involve seeing the look of satisfaction on a student's face as she held up a new creation.

I hope this book will bring you many hours of pleasure. Increase your satisfaction by making the projects your own with your favorite colors. You'll cherish these jewelry pieces because they'll work with everything in your wardrobe and never go out of style. Add some crystals and they'll be sparkly additions to evening wear. And because they're your very own creations, they'll add to your feelings of pride and self-confidence.

Enjoy your beading!

Diane M. Fitzgerald

Foreword
by Jean Campbell

"I'll call Diane. She'll know."

I've uttered this phrase many times in the years I've known Diane Fitzgerald. She is *the* go-to beader. A consummate maven of the bead world. A talented scholar, designer, and teacher. One of the cornerstones of modern beading. Lofty accolades, right? But as you page through these wonderful projects, which she's taught over the years, I think you'll feel the sense of creative strength and design knowledge for which Diane has rightly earned these words of praise.

Diane is the person I call when I have a question about the history of beadwork, a query about a product, or a teaching question. Her down-to-earth Midwestern roots make her approachable and funny, but her quest for knowledge makes her a walking bead encyclopedia.

The Scholar

Diane had a twenty-year career in public relations before discovering beading. Though she enjoyed needlepoint and quilting, when she attended a class on needleweaving with Helen Banes in 1989, she felt she'd found her creative niche. She immediately immersed herself in the art, taking classes from some of the greats—Virginia Blakelock, Carol Perrenoud, Horace Goodhue, and Joyce Scott. Also in 1989, Diane couldn't resist purchasing an entire stash of beads from a fellow beader. The acquisition put her into the bead business and she opened

her shop, Beautiful Beads, in Minneapolis. By 1995, Diane was a contributing editor to *Bead&Button* magazine, was writing *Beads and Threads* with Helen Banes, founding the Upper Midwest Bead Society in Minneapolis, and doing lots of teaching.

In person, you can tell Diane's been captured by the bead sirens. For one, she's usually festooned with an elaborate beaded necklace of her own design. Her eyes absolutely sparkle at the mention of a beaderly subject she hasn't encountered before. When I first met Diane, she was dissecting an old piece of African Zulu beadwork to analyze how the stitch was done; she told me at length how amazed she was at the ingenuity of the maker. That fervor for knowledge leads Diane in dozens of directions, whether figuring out an ancient stitch or finding out how a particular bead was manufactured. For instance, Diane loves

Two-Hole Bead Necklace in Black and Copper, 2004
52 CM LONG

Pressed glass beads; netting

Two-hole beads have long been a collecting niche for Diane. They were popular from the '20s through the '50s, but you can still find stashes of old ones. This style of necklace would have been popular in the 1940s.

Needlewoven Necklace with Scarab Buckle, 1991
14 X 17 CM

Fiber, vintage scarab buckle, pressed glass beads; needleweaving

Diane's start in beading began with a class in needlewoven necklaces taught by Helen Banes, and the two later co-authored a how-to book. Diane used this technique to make this necklace featuring a vintage Egyptian Revival scarab buckle as the central motif and vintage glass teardrop pendants as accents.

Morroccan Lanterns Necklace, 2009
61 CM LONG

Delica beads, vintage nailheads, Nymo D thread, metal chain; peyote stitch

Sometimes, students help Diane name pieces. In the case of this necklace, a student in England said she'd seen a picture of Moroccan lanterns in a magazine and the pendants in this necklace reminded her of them.

two-holed beads. She collects antique ones from 1920s to 1950s Czechoslovakia and has written several articles about them, and her love of them led her to dive, head-first, into learning about the new Japanese Tila two-hole beads. She embraced this new product with new techniques and published projects.

Diane's ravenous appetite for bead knowledge has taken her to 38 countries. She's written extensively about her quest, bringing readers along on her travels to places from a Marrakech souk to London's Portobello Road. Diane has taught about Egyptian revival jewelry, Zulu girls' initiation ceremonies, and modern American art glass beads. Among other things, she's taught the best way to haggle for Berber beads, explained how to identify authentic Bohemian peacock eye beads, and given us an inside look at the Miyuki bead factory.

The Designer

Lucky for us, Diane brings her travel discoveries directly back to her design studio. She uses the whole world as her inspiration. This is clear in her Moroccan Lanterns Necklace. The strand is decorated with ornate beaded pendants that evoke something that might hang in a sheik's tent.

Diane's work with the Zulu beadwork of South Africa gave her a rich field from which to work. She learned dozens of Zulu beading techniques and used them to make beautiful and contemporary pieces, like the African Circle Stitch Necklace and Flowerette Bracelet. By incorporating Austrian crystal and metal-plated beads, Diane elevated these ancient tribal techniques to haute couture.

In Diane's Mexican Fiesta Bracelet, dramatic netting increases summon to mind

Mexican Fiesta Bracelet, 1992

4 X 19.5 X 2.5 CM

Seed beads; netting

Czechoslovakia was the fountainhead of beads in the first half of the twentieth century. During this period, many women made extra money working at home stringing beads for local factories. They used a simple machine much like a potter's wheel. As a large round tray rotated from the operation of foot pedals, the stringer would insert several very long threaded needles into it. Almost instantly, the needles would be full of beads and the stringer would slip them onto thread to be measured and tied into hanks. Here, Diane tries her hand at bead stringing, but quickly finds out what skill it takes.

Photo by Christa Petraskova

the colorful, swirling skirts of Mexican folkloric dancers. To wear a bracelet like this is to wear the mood and movement of an experience. This bracelet is another great example of how Diane works "new" just about every time she makes something. She responds to experiences first, only depending on her established style once she has uncovered the mood of her experience.

The Teacher

The way Diane shares her knowledge of beads with such gusto is what draws so many students to her. Whether it's through her numerous books, articles, or workshops, she's a tireless educator, encouraging the joy and creativity that comes from beadwork.

In the late 1990s, when I was editor of *Beadwork* magazine and Diane a regular contributor, we had many serious discussions about elevating the bead community's knowledge overall. I laugh now about how we'd argue about the proper

Diane in 2007, decked out in full kimono regalia in Tokyo's famous Takashimaya department store.

Photo by Jeannette Cook

use of words in beading instructions, as we both hoped for an easy, universal beading language. During this time Diane constantly reminded me to cater not only to advanced beadworkers, but to help out the beginners, too. Her influence pushed me to make sure we helped newcomers learn the basic stitches through special techniques sections and easier projects. It's interesting to look back now and realize that Diane's influence definitely made an impact—the number of beaders in the last 15 or so years has easily tripled.

Diane continues to act as an enthusiastic teacher through her magazine articles and lectures, whether about designing beadwork, working with color, or getting the most out of a beading class. She has even taught bead teachers how to be more effective. She wants to share everything she's learned to boost the whole community, exciting us all to become more involved.

The crown of Diane's career, however, has to be her workshops. She has taught extensively throughout the United States, the United Kingdom, Japan, and Germany. She's in constant demand because she encourages her students to find their own voices through creative play. When teaching a pattern, she comes armed with many examples to spark creative confidence in her students, motivating them to try a little design work on their own.

So here, you have 24 of this bead maven's favorite class projects. Working through any of these projects might feel like attending a special Diane Fitzgerald workshop, but in the comfort of your bead studio. In doing so, you join the thousands of other students in Diane's workshops who have enjoyed the knowledge, inspiration, and joy she brings to everything she does.

African Circle Stitch Necklace, 2006

34 X 13.5 CM

Seed beads, crystals; African circle stitch

When she was invited to teach for Swarovski in Japan, Diane asked her host what he'd like her to teach. At that time, she had made only a few pieces with crystals. After thinking for a moment, her host responded, "I would like you to take the Zulu techniques in your book, *Zulu Inspired Beadwork*, and make them with crystals." It was a brilliant idea! This necklace was the result.

Flowerette Bracelet, 2007

23.2 CM LONG

Crystals, charlottes, cube beads; Zulu-inspired technique

The beading techniques of the Zulu people of South Africa are among the most intricate in the world. This popular Zulu pattern takes on an entirely new look when crystals are used instead of seed beads.

One-to-Many Strand

Necklace

The One-to-Many Strand Necklace can have from 10 to 20 strands of multicolored seed beads, small stone chips, and small beads supported by a single strand of large bold beads on each side. The texture created by the multicolored seed beads and small beads contrasts with the bold large beads to make this necklace a striking piece that will never go out of style. Color mixing with seed beads, a process akin to mixing paint, is an important part of creating this necklace.

SUPPLIES

Mixed shades of red and turquoise 9° to 15° round or cut seed beads, approximately 85 g*

200–300 small beads, small stone chips, rondelles, and size 8° or 6° seed beads, in colors coordinating with the 9° to 15° seed beads

2 brass round decorative beads, 20 mm

6 red cube beads, 12 x 12 x 10 mm

6 brass ribbed bicone spacers, 6 mm

2 turquoise glass oval beads, 10 x 25 mm

2 red glass faceted round beads, 10 mm

2 turquoise glass round beads, 12 mm

2 light turquoise glass bicones, 10 mm

2 turquoise glass round beads, 8 mm

10 bronze cubes, 3 mm

Necklace clasp

2 clamshell bead tips

1½ yards (1.4 m) of #18 nylon cord or size F or FF nylon bead cord**

Tape

Piece of cardboard, 12 x 18 inches (30.5 x 46 cm)

Nylon beading thread, size D

Scissors

Size 12 beading needles

Microcrystalline wax

Disposable lighter

Clear nail polish

Pencil and paper

Small box lid or bottom about 4 x 4 x 1 inch (10 x 10 x 2.5 cm) deep

*See the Selecting Colors tip box

**Sometimes used in upholstery and called #18 cord

Dimensions: 26¾ inches (68 cm) long

1 Mix your 9° to 15° seed beads together in a small dish by adding about half a spoonful at a time and watching how the color mixture shifts. (Remember—it's easy to mix beads, but difficult to separate them again, so add small amounts each time.) Place your small beads, stone chips, rondelles, or size 6° or 8° seed beads in coordinating colors in a dish nearby.

2 Refer to **FIGURE 1** as you work steps 2 through 4. Cut 2 pieces of size F or FF nylon bead cord, each 24 inches (61 cm) long. Fold each in half. Place them on the cardboard so the folded ends are 13½ inches (34.5 cm) apart and are pointing toward each other. Tape the cord securely to the cardboard. The strands of seed beads and small beads will be strung back and forth between these 2 loops. Adjust this length if you wish.

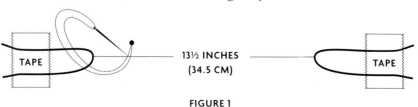

TAPE

13½ INCHES
(34.5 CM)

TAPE

FIGURE 1

3 Thread a beading needle with 3 yards (2.7 m) of
size D nylon thread, bring the ends together, wax
well so that the strands adhere to each other like
a single strand, and knot with an overhand knot
(FIGURE 2). Clip the tail 1 mm from the knot and melt
the knot slightly with a disposable lighter. (Don't put
the tails in the flame, just near it.) Check to make
sure the knot is secure.

FIGURE 2

4 Attach the thread to 1 cord loop with a lark's
head or sales tag knot, as follows: Pass the needle
through one of the cord loops. Bring the knotted end
of the thread near the cord loop. Separate the strands
between the knot and the cord loop. Pass the needle
between the two strands and pull it so the knot is
next to the bead cord **(FIGURE 3)**.

FIGURE 3

5 Put the seed beads in the box lid and slide them
toward one corner. Add seed beads by scooping
them onto the needle by passing the needle through
the mound of beads with a slight upward motion
like an airplane taking off. After each needleful—or
about every 1¼ inches (3 cm) of seed beads—add a
stone chip or a bead that's larger than the seed beads.

adding new thread

When you run out of thread, add more in the
middle of an existing strand, not near the loops.
Here's how: Leave the old needle on the thread.
Prepare a second threaded needle as you did in step
3. Pass the new needle through the last 4 to 6 beads
just strung so that both needles are exiting the
same bead and in the same direction. Tie the old
and new threads together with a square knot. Apply clear nail polish
to the knot. String more beads onto the new thread. Later, to hide the
old thread, pass through several beads, tie an overhand knot between
the beads, pass through a few more beads, and clip.

When the length of the strand is exactly long enough to reach
the loop of the second cord, pass the needle through the loop
and back through the last 2 or 3 beads just strung (going in the
opposite direction) as shown in **FIGURE 4**. Avoid adding a small
bead near the cord loops because it will interfere with the way the
strands hang. Continue going back and forth until you have the
desired number of strands for your necklace, anywhere from 10
to 20 strands.

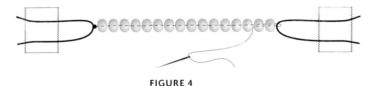

FIGURE 4

6 After the desired number of strands are strung, remove the
tape from the bead cord on one end and string on the 6 to 7
inches (15.2 to 17.8 cm) of large, bold beads on the strands (both
strands go through the beads). Bring the 2 ends of the bead cord
through a bead tip. Tie the 2 ends together with a square knot and
apply nail polish to the knot. Clip the excess cord. Squeeze the
2 halves of the bead tip over the knot with pliers to close the tip
(FIGURE 5). Do the same with the cord on the other side. Attach 1
part of the clasp to each bead tip.

FIGURE 5

Choose large, bold, solid color beads that
will string up to a length of about 6½ inches
(16.5 cm) for each end of the necklace.

Create a sensuous necklace by tying beads together rather than simply stringing them, and by attaching strands of beads, also by tying them on. Larger elements with two holes work well to bring this style together. Dangling cord ends are part of the design, adding a softness and tendril-like feel. You may not find elements exactly like those used here, so be prepared to experiment with your materials in whatever way necessary. Just "tie one on!"

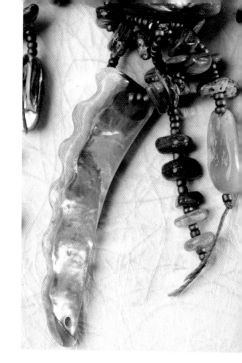

Tie-One-On Necklace

SUPPLIES

Conso #18 nylon cord in a color that works with your beads, or size FF or FFF nylon bead cord*

Beads for the "backbone," about 5 to 11 flat pieces with 1 large or 2 small holes, such as donuts

Chips or small beads; other dangles (optional)

Japanese seed beads in colors related to your larger beads, size 6° to 11°, with holes large enough to string on #18 cord, 5 to 10 g

Button, bead, or toggle for the clasp

1 heavy straight pin or T-pin

Clear nail polish

Disposable lighter

Towel, placemat, or other work surface

*Sometimes used in upholstery and called #18 cord

Dimensions: 3⅛ x 26 inches (8 x 66 cm)

1 Begin by laying out the major components on your work surface, arranging them as you envision them in your necklace. Then sprinkle seed beads, small beads, and chips between them to see the overall effect.

2 Join large components with one of the knots—the overhand knot, square knot, or lark's head knot **(FIGURES 1 TO 3)**. Cut a length of bead cord about 12 to 15 inches (30 to 38 cm) and apply clear nail polish to the ends to stiffen them. Join

FIGURE 1

FIGURE 2

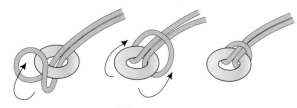

FIGURE 3

2 components with this thread (FIGURE 4), stringing seed beads, small beads, and/or chips to cover the cord. Space the components about 1 to 1½ inches (2.5 to 4 cm) apart. Bring the cord ends together and tie with an overhand knot. Attach seed beads and chips or other dangles to the ends of the cord. Finish the end of the cord with an overhand knot to prevent the beads from falling off. Melt the end with a lighter or let it fray.

3 Add other dangles with a lark's head knot and finish the ends as above.

4 For the clasp or closure, tie a button, bead, or toggle to your last component. Finish the ends as above. For the other side, tie a loop to the last component and wrap it with the buttonhole stitch (FIGURE 5).

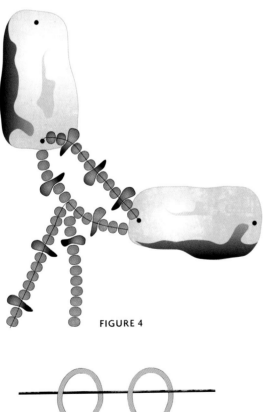

FIGURE 4

FIGURE 5

Shimmering
Waves Necklace

This delicate necklace will bring rave reviews. The chain is a typical zigzag chain worked back and forth, similar to peyote, but with a picot, which is an extra bead on the outer edge of each side. Add a button at the center to serve as a focal point.

SUPPLIES

A, size 11° cylinder beads, 15 g*

B, size 15° seed beads, 7 g

1 snap, ¼ inch (6 mm) in diameter

1 button, ⅞ inch (2.2 cm) in diameter

Nylon beading thread, size D, in a color to match the beads

Size 10 or 12 beading needle

*Or 5 g each of 3 colors close in value and hue. For an interesting variegated effect that gives wonderful highlights and shadows, use 3 shades of a single color of cylinder beads, such as metallic, silver-lined, and semi-matte silver-lined or iridescent. Begin with about 30 cylinder beads of 1 color, then make a gradual transition to the second color by mixing 8 to 10 beads of each color and adding them at random. Continue with the second color until there are 8 to 10 beads left, then mix these with 8 to 10 beads of the third color, and so on.

Dimensions: 18⅛ inches (46 cm) long

1 Thread the needle with 1½ yards (1.4 m) of thread. String 2 A, 1 B, and 2 A. Tie these 5 beads into a tight ring, leaving a 4-inch (10 cm) tail **(FIGURE 1)**.

2 Add 2 A, 1 B, and 2 A. Pass back through 2 A in the first 5-bead ring **(FIGURE 2)**.

3 Add 1 B and 2 A. Pass back through the last 2 A added in the previous step **(FIGURE 3)**. Continue to repeat this step for the desired length **(FIGURE 4)**. Keep your tension tight. For an 18-inch (45.5 cm) necklace, make 2 strips with 312 picots on each. For a longer necklace, each additional 12 beads will add approximately ¾ inch (2 cm).

4 Make the S-curve as follows: When the chain is the desired length, knot the thread between the last A and B. Pass

through 12 B on one side of the band. Pass through 4 A to the other side of the band **(FIGURE 5)**. Pull the thread tight so the band curves. Knot between the beads. Continue passing through 12 B on one side, then passing through 4 A to the other side, then knotting and passing through 12 B again.

5 After completing the S-curve band, align the ends of the 2 bands at one end and stitch them together. Intertwine the bands so they cross and wrap around one another and lie flat. Stitch the bands together at the intersections, passing through the beads or around the thread if the bead holes are full.

6 Sew 1 side of the snap to each end of the necklace.

7 Sew the button to the center of the necklace.

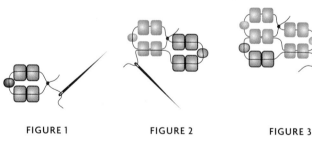

FIGURE 1   FIGURE 2   FIGURE 3   FIGURE 4

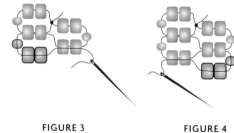

FIGURE 5

Miriam Haskell's designs were worn by movie stars, such as Lucille Ball, Myrna Loy, and Joan Crawford. Today, her pieces are among the most collectible in costume jewelry and command high prices at antique shows. Much of Haskell's work features beads attached to a perforated metal plate and components covered with tiny seed beads. Accordingly, the pins in this project involve wiring beads to a foundation. Studying her work, the work of her famous contemporaries Robert DeMario and Stanley Hagler, and later designers such as Ian St. Gielar—to name just a few—can provide inspiration and a starting point for your own creations.

Collage Pin

SUPPLIES

Spool of 28-gauge brass wire

6 large filigree leaves

Assortment of components*

1 pin back

Wire cutters

Pencil and paper

Chain-nose pliers

Dapping block and dapping tool

*See page 24

Dimensions: 3⅛ x 3⅛ inches (8 x 8 cm)

Getting Started

If you look closely at jewelry designed by Miriam Haskell and others of her time period, you'll notice in many cases that components are layered to create a rich and varied collage. Some are only partly exposed and seem to peek out from beneath other ones, while others nestle within each other like a set of Russian dolls. These components may include wheels with rhinestones, cross-hole petal and leaf beads wired into rings, metal leaves or flower shapes wrapped with seed beads or tiny pearls, flower beads layered on beaded flower petals or filigree metal stampings, and charms or buttons, among many others. Begin with an idea, a theme, or a sketch of what you'd like to make. Next, go through your beads, buttons, and findings and gather what you'd like to work with. Your selection should be based on your theme or on a palette of colors, or possibly even on shapes. Look for components with holes going crosswise rather than lengthwise; they're easier to wire on securely. Depending on how elaborate you want your own pin to look, you

▲ Instead of making a filigree backing, you could use commercial findings for a collage pin. These include, clockwise from top left, a back plate with the pin back soldered on, a finding that converts a pin into a pendant, the front of a back plate, and a perforated plate to which elements are wired. The perforated plate is inserted into the front of the back plate, with the prongs closed around it to hold it in place.

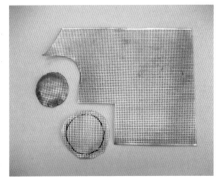

▲ If you can't find filigree leaves or a commercial finding in the size and shape you want, you can cut your own shape from perforated brass sheet using metal shears.

might also round up shank buttons, pearls, rose montées, memory wire, bead caps, crystal head pins, chain, jump rings, charms, filigree components, shells, stones, junk jewelry or broken trinkets, watch parts, single earrings (which can be the starting point for a great pin), and other found objects—as well as a digital camera, which is useful for recording designs.

Before you begin to assemble the pin, you should also make several components from the beads in your palette so you won't have to stop to make an element and can easily try out different colors and shapes as you layer on the beads. Instructions for a variety of components start on page 24. These instructions explain the basic steps in creating a collage pin or pendant on a constructed filigree backing or a perforated plate with a back. Feel free to experiment with different backings and components. The technique is simple, but your eye for arrangement is what makes the brooch beautiful and unique.

1 Wire together 3 filigree leaf shapes. These will be used for the front of the pin. Trace the outline of their shape onto paper. Dap them slightly so that they are slightly concave (PHOTO 1).

2 Working on the paper tracing, try out various arrangements of the components you've gathered.

It may be handy to take a picture with a digital camera so that you can re-create a favorite composition.

3 Attach the components to the trio of filigree leaves. The components must be absolutely tight so they don't move. A wobbly component will have to be reinforced or reworked. Begin by cutting several 3- to 4-inch (7.5 to 10 cm) lengths of 28-gauge wire (so that you won't have to stop to cut more wire as you work).

Ideally, it's best to wire each component to the perforated plate in 2 places, or in other words, to attach the component with wire through 2 holes. With the wires exiting the back of the plate, cross the left wire over the right one, with the wires crossing at a right angle like a plus sign. At the point where the wires cross, grab them with the tip of the chain-nose pliers and twist once to the right (FIGURE 1). Then move the pliers down the wires closer to the plate and twist to the right again. Make sure the wires still cross at right angles. Don't simply twist one wire around the other (FIGURE 2). Repeat

PHOTO 1

FIGURE 1

until you're certain the component is held firmly in place and the wires are twisted properly. Later, the wires will be clipped about ⅜ inch (1 cm) from the plate and folded toward the plate (PHOTO 2). For now, leave them uncut because you may wish to twist these wires together with other wires.

Sometimes the wire breaks and you have to start over. It takes a bit of practice to become good at this, so be patient until you gain some experience.

4 Wire together 3 filigree leaf shapes in a configuration identical to the one made in step 1. This will be the back of the pin. Wire a pin back to it (PHOTO 3).

5 Wire the front of the pin to the back of the pin, wrong sides together (PHOTO 4). Tuck the wire ends between the front and back plates.

PHOTO 3

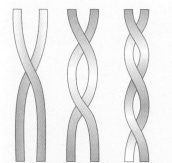

Correct: The twist begins with a crossed pair, with the wires tightened progressively.

Incorrect: One wire is straight, with the other wire twisted around it. The straight wire has no holding power.

FIGURE 2

PHOTO 4

PHOTO 2

▲ A dapping block is a cube of hardwood 2 x 2 x 2 inches (5 x 5 x 5 cm) with domed depressions of various sizes on each side. Use it to shape filigree pieces or perforated brass sheet into a dome shape that will accommodate and hide the wire used to hold components in place.

Components

FLOWER PETALS OR LEAVES

Petal and leaf sets are quick to make using petal-shaped beads with cross holes. String between 5 and 7 beads onto a 4-inch (10 cm) length of 28-gauge wire. Push the beads to the center of the wire so that all the beads are touching. Cross the wires as close to the beads as possible, then grab the wires where they cross with the tip of your chain-nose pliers. Twist several times to tighten. Leave on the wire ends to attach the set to the perforated base **(PHOTO 5)**.

These sets can be layered or stacked with buttons, bead caps, crystal head pins, or other flat beads, and then attached to the perforated base.

Sometimes you'll have just 2 or 3 flower petal or leaf beads left. You can use these to make a partial flower that peeks out from behind a larger flower.

LEAVES WITH SERRATED EDGES

The vintage metal leaves with serrated edges used in Haskell's jewelry are hard to find, so I have developed a substitute. The leaves allow you to easily introduce color and shapes to enhance your design because they have seed beads wrapped around them.

Trace the template below onto shrink plastic, then cut the pattern with scissors that have notched blades. Punch a ⅛-inch (3 mm) hole, then shrink, following the manufacturer's instructions **(PHOTO 6)**. For a metallic look, use a gold or silver paint pen to color the edge of the leaves after shrinking them.

BEAD-WRAPPED LEAVES

Leaves with serrated edges can be wrapped with seed beads; the serrated edge holds the wire in place. The texture of the seed beads contrasts nicely with the smooth texture of large glass beads and metal elements.

String 3 to 4 inches (7.5 to 10 cm) of size 11° seed beads onto 28-gauge wire that's still on the spool. Insert the end of the wire into the hole of the leaf, leaving a 1-inch (2.5 cm) tail. Wrap the wire once around the leaf stem. Pass 2 beads next to the leaf edge and bring the wire around the back and to the front again so that the 2 beads are positioned on the front of the leaf. Continue to add as many beads as necessary to reach across the leaf horizontally, then bring the wire around the back. When adding the last row of 1 or 2 beads, wrap the wire around the stem, then back to the tip, add the beads, then wrap around the stem again. Clip the wire and twist the wire ends together **(PHOTO 7)**.

TEMPLATE, ACTUAL SIZE

PHOTO 5

PHOTO 6

PHOTO 7

The Yao are an East African ethnic group living in southern Malawi. They produce a variety of colorful arts and crafts, such as wood and soapstone carvings, traditional musical instruments, textiles, pottery, beadwork, and baskets. This simple band necklace is adapted from a Yao child's necklace.

The project offers a great opportunity to study color interaction. Four color shades are recommended: dark, medium, light, and bright. This necklace is understated and can be worn easily with simple shirts, turtlenecks, and casual clothes.

Yao Necklace

SUPPLIES

A, light color size 11° Japanese seed beads, 13 g

B, medium color size 11° Japanese seed beads, 13 g

C, dark color size 11° Japanese seed beads, 13 g

D, bright color size 11° Japanese seed beads, 13 g

2 buttons, ³⁄₈ inch (1 cm) in diameter, for the closure

1 accent pendant, button, or large bead (optional)

Nylon beading thread, size D

Size 12 beading needles

Scissors

Dimensions: *24 inches (61 cm) long*

You can make this design any length, or even shorten it for a bracelet. The basic unit of the band **(FIGURE 8)** is made of 4 rows of square stitch followed by 5 single-needle ladder tabs. It may be made with a button and loop closure at the back or without a closure. The 2 sides of the band are joined in the center with a V-shaped section of square stitch accented with a small pendant bead or beads.

Square Stitch Section

Thread a needle with 1½ yards (1.4 m) of thread, single. String on a stopper bead, which will be removed later, then pass through the bead again **(FIGURE 1)**.

Row 1: Add 13 A **(FIGURE 1, BLUE LINE)**.

Row 2: Add 1 B. Pass through the last bead added in the previous row from left to right, then through the new bead **(FIGURE 1, RED LINE)**.

FIGURE 1

FIGURE 2

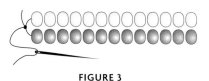

FIGURE 3

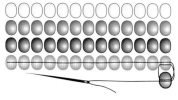

FIGURE 4

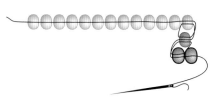

FIGURE 5

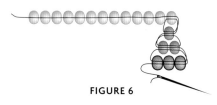

FIGURE 6

Add 1 B. Pass through the last 2 beads of the previous row from left to right, then through the 2 beads of the new row **(FIGURE 2).**

Work across the row: Add 1 B, and, moving over 1 bead in the previous row, pass through 2 beads and then through the last 2 beads in the new row.

At the end of the row, remove the stopper bead and tie the working thread to the tail **(FIGURE 3).**

Rows 3 and 4: Turn and work 2 more rows as you did in Row 2, using C and then D.

Single-Needle Ladder Tab Section

Make a tab using colors as you wish.

Row 1: Add 1 bead. Pass through the last bead of the previous row from left to right, then through the new bead **(FIGURE 4).**

Row 2: Add 2 beads. Pass through the single bead added in Row 1, then through the 2 new beads **(FIGURE 5).**

Rows 3–8: Add 3 beads. Pass through the beads added in the previous row, then through the 3 new beads **(FIGURE 6).**

Row 9: Add 2 beads. Pass through the beads added in the previous row, then through the 2 new beads.

Row 10: Add 1 bead. Pass through the beads added in the previous row, then through the new bead.

Pass the thread back and forth through all rows of this tab until you reach the first bead added in this section. Pass

through the beads of the last row of square stitch so your thread is exiting the fourth bead from the right **(FIGURE 7).**

Make 4 more tabs. (On the remaining tabs, skip 3 beads between tabs.)

On the last tab, do not pass back up through the beads to the beginning of the tab.

Join the Tabs to the Next Square Stitch Section

Turn the work so you're working right to left. Add 1 bead, pass through the last bead of the last tab, then through the new bead again.

Add 3 beads. Pass through the last bead of the next tab from left to right and through the new bead again **(FIGURE 8).** Repeat this step 3 more times.

Work 10 Square Stitch and Single-Needle Ladder sections for each side of the necklace by repeating the instructions from Row 2 of the Square Stitch Section to this point 10 times.

Join the Bands

After completing the last tab of the second band, continue with the same thread. Join the tabs of the first band to a row of square stitch as described above. Add 3 beads and begin to join the tabs of the second band.

Make the finishing triangle, as follows: Work square stitch back and forth as described in the Square Stitch Section, but decrease 1 bead at the beginning and end of each row until there is only 1 bead at the bottom **(FIGURE 9).**

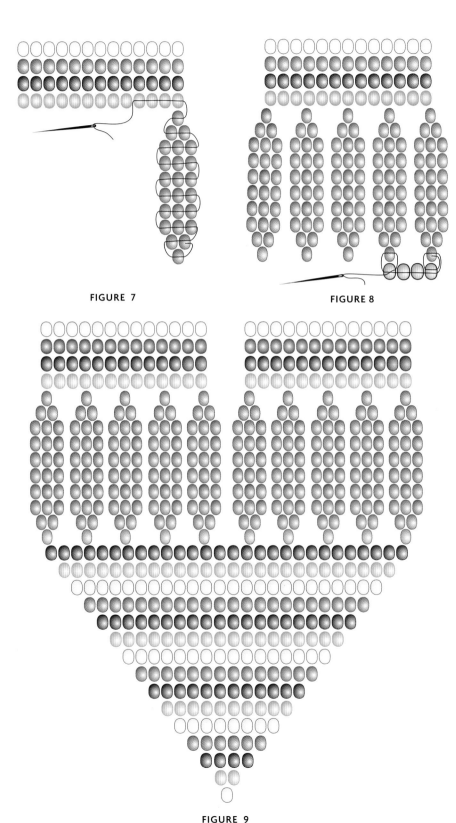

FIGURE 7

FIGURE 8

FIGURE 9

Add the Pendant

For a cross-hole pendant, with thread exiting the tip bead of the triangle, add enough size 11° seed beads to reach the hole of the pendant bead. Pass through the pendant. Add the same number of size 11° seed beads less one again and pass through the first size 11° seed bead and then through the triangle tip bead **(FIGURE 10)**.

For a vertical-hole pendant, pass through the pendant bead, add 1 size 11° seed bead, and pass back through the pendant bead and the tip bead of the triangle from the opposite side **(FIGURE 11)**.

Knot the thread and weave in the tail.

Attach the Closure

To make the closure, sew 2 buttons to the middle row of the left band.

Sew 2 loops of size 11° seed beads to the middle row of the right band. Begin and end the loop by going through the same bead **(FIGURE 12)**.

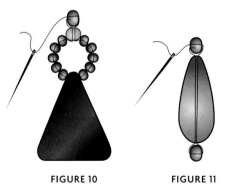

FIGURE 10

FIGURE 11

FIGURE 12

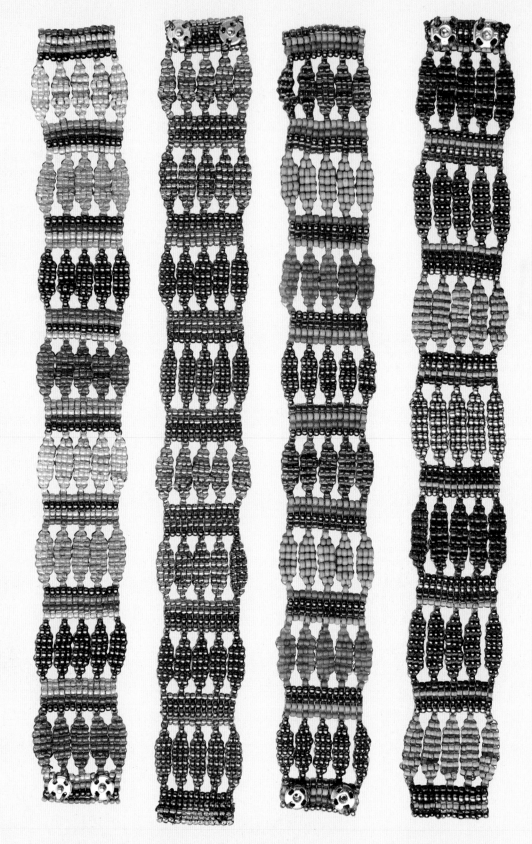

A bracelet requires 5 g of size 11° Japanese seed beads in each of 4 colors, as well as 2 snaps for the closure. Work 1 band to the desired length, ending with a square stitch section. Sew snaps to each end of the band.

Merry Cherries Necklace

Merry Cherries
Necklace

If you loved the Bakelite cherry necklaces of the 1930s, you'll want to make this sparkling version with bicone crystals and cylinder bead leaves suspended from a metal chain.

SUPPLIES

A, dark green opaque size 11° cylinder beads, 6 g

B, leaf green opaque size 11° cylinder beads, 9 g

C, semi-matte silver-lined red size 11° cylinder beads, 4 g

D, 300 light Siam crystal bicones, 5 mm

18 inches (46 cm) of dark metal chain with large links

1 dark metal clasp

15 dark metal split rings, 6 mm

1 yard (91.5 cm) of black waxed cord, 2 mm

Green Nymo beading thread, size D

Crystal Fireline braided beading thread, 6 lb.

Scissors

Microcrystalline wax

Size 12 beading needles

2 pairs of needle-nose pliers

Disposable lighter

Pledge with Future Finish Floor Polish (optional)

Dimensions: *17 inches (43 cm) long*

Leaves

Leaves are formed with green cylinder beads and peyote stitch, working first along 1 side of the center spine and then the other. Make 10 leaves.

1 With 1½ yards (1.4 m) of single Nymo D thread, tie 1 A on the end of the thread (this bead will be left in your work) leaving a 3- to 4-inch (7.5 to 10 cm) tail. To form the spine, string on 35 more A. Pass back through the second-to-last bead added, forming the tip end **(FIGURE 1)**.

2 Work peyote stitch toward the opposite (stem) end, as follows: Add 1 A and pass through the second bead along the strand, counting from where your thread exited a bead. Continue to the end of the row. End exiting the tied-on A bead. Tie the working thread to the tail. The spine is now complete **(FIGURE 2)**.

3 Turn and, without adding a bead, pass through the last bead added **(FIGURE 2)**. You're now ready to begin Row 1.

4 Work back and forth across the spine in peyote stitch according to the pattern. At the end of each row, turn and, without adding a bead, pass through the last bead added **(FIGURE 3)**. When you complete Row 10, there will be 7 beads sticking up on one side of the leaf. Pass the thread through the beads to the stem end of the spine.

Row 1: (First row after the spine worked in peyote stitch) *Stitch 2 B, 1 A,* then repeat from * to * 4 more times, then 1 B.

Row 2: Stitch 3 B, then stitch *1 A, 2 B* 4 times.

FIGURE 1

FIGURE 2

Row 3: Stitch *2 B, 1 A,* then repeat from * to * 3 more times, then 2 B.

Row 4: Stitch 1 B, then stitch *1 A, 2 B*, and repeat from * to * 3 more times.

Row 5: Stitch *2 B, 1 A,* then repeat from * to * 2 more times, then 3 B.

Row 6: Stitch *2 B, 1 A,* then repeat from * to * 2 more times, then 2 B.

Row 7: Stitch *2 B, 1 A,* then repeat from * to * 2 more times, then 1 B.

Row 8: Stitch 3 B, then stitch *1 A, 2 B* 2 times.

Row 9: Stitch 8 B.

Row 10: Stitch 7 B.

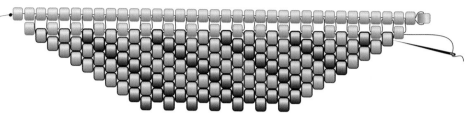

FIGURE 3

5 Attach the split ring as follows: Sew the split ring to the stem end bead before beginning the second side of the leaf, stitching through the stem end bead and the split ring several times. Then continue with the second side of the leaf. Pass through the tied-on bead and exit the second bead from the stem end on the opposite side of the spine. Work along the spine on the other side, following the pattern for Rows 1 to 10.

Weave in the tail threads and clip the tails. If you wish to stiffen the leaf, dip it in Pledge with Future Finish Floor Polish. Lay it flat to dry on waxed paper.

Cherries

To make the cherry, we'll begin by making a strip with bicones and cylinder beads, then the ends of the strip will be connected to form a ring. The top of the ring will be filled in with 5 bicones and cylinder beads, forming a star with 5 rays. Then the thread is passed to the bottom side of the ring and finished like the top. Just before completing the last star center in the bottom, the stem will be inserted so that the knot in the end of the stem is inside the cherry. I suggest you be very patient as you make your cherries. Take your time. Work slowly. Draw the thread

through the beads very slowly to prevent tangling. Don't allow the thread to get kinks in it. Make sure it pulls all the way through the beads and that no loops are formed.

Prepare the Stems: Cut the waxed cord into 5 equal pieces, each about 7 inches (18 cm) long. String 1 split ring onto the center of the cord and tie a single knot around it. Make an overhand knot 1½ inches (4 cm) away from the center. Clip off the tails, leaving ¼ inch (6 mm) below the knot. Make sure the knot is tight.

Prepare the Thread: Thread a needle with 3 yards (2.7 m) of Fireline thread. Bring the ends together. Wax the thread several times with the microcrystalline wax so the strands adhere to each other like a single strand. Knot the ends together with an overhand knot. Clip the tails close to the knot and melt the knot slightly with a disposable lighter. Don't put the knot in the flame, just near it. Test the knot by pulling on it to make sure it is secure.

In the diagrams on the next couple of pages, new beads and new thread paths are shown with a bold line.

To begin, count 1 pile of 20 bicones, and 2 piles of 5 bicones each. Keep tension as tight as possible by pulling thread in the direction of the stitch.

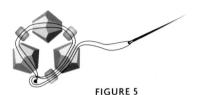

FIGURE 4

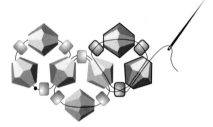

FIGURE 5

FIGURE 6

FIGURE 7

34

1 Add 1 D and 1 C 3 times **(FIGURE 4)**.

2 Pass the beads to within 1 inch (2.5 cm) of the knot. Separate the threads between the beads and the knot. Pass the needle between the threads. Pass back through the first C and D next to it **(FIGURE 5)**.

3 Add 1 C and 1 D twice, then add 1 C. Pass through the D just exited from the opposite end **(FIGURE 6, RED LINE)**.

4 Continue through the next C and the next D to the right **(FIGURE 6, RED LINE)**.

5 Add 1 C and 1 D twice, then add 1 C. Pass through the D just exited from the opposite end. Continue through the next C and D to the right **(FIGURE 7)**.

triangle weave rule

Triangle beadwork is much like right angle weave. You can only pass your needle through the bead directly to the right or left of the bead your thread is exiting.

6 Repeat steps 3 to 5 three more times. Your piece should look like **FIGURE 8**. Lay it out in front of you so the knot is on the lower left and the needle is exiting a D on the upper right. Now look carefully at **FIGURE 8**. Note that there are 5 D sitting horizontally across the top and 4 D sitting horizontally across the bottom of the strip. Between these horizontal rows of D there are D that sit diagonally. The ends of the strip will now be joined to form a ring.

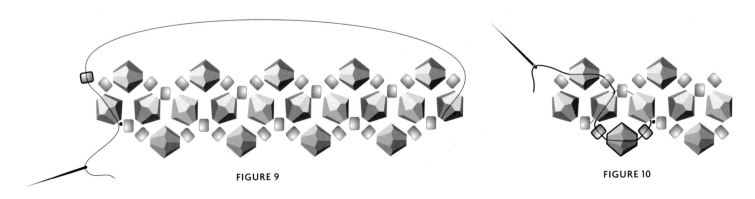

FIGURE 8

FIGURE 9

FIGURE 10

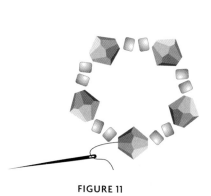

FIGURE 11

FIGURE 12

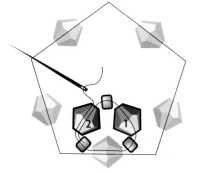

FIGURE 13

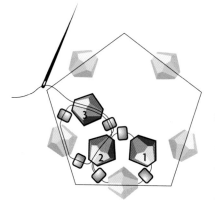

FIGURE 14

Want a matching brooch? Just make a pair of leaves, stitch them together, add a couple of cherries, and sew on a pin back.

7 Add 1 C and pass through the first diagonal D at the beginning of the strip **(FIGURE 9)**.

8 Add 1 C, 1 D, and 1 C. Pass through the D just exited at the end of the strip (this closes the strip and forms a ring). Then pass through the next C to the left and the next D to the left **(FIGURE 10)**.

9 Look at the ring from the top down. Make sure you can identify 5 D along the rim and that your thread is exiting a D from right to left as shown **(FIGURE 11)**. Now we'll begin to build the bottom of the cherry as shown above by adding 5 D

with a C in between. Count out 5 D and 15 C. These will be used for the bottom of the cherry **(FIGURE 12)**.

10 Add 1 C and 1 D twice (#1 and #2), then add 1 more C. Pass through the D just exited in the ring, the next C, and the next D **(FIGURE 13)**.

11 Add 1 C, 1 D (#3), and 1 C. Pass through the next bicone on the ring toward the bead you exited at the beginning of this step. Add 1 C and pass through the D just exited, the next C, and the next D **(FIGURE 14)**.

12 Add 1 C and pass through the next D on the ring. Add 1 C, 1 D, and 1 C, and pass through the D exited from the center toward the outer ring. Continue through the C, the D in the ring, the C, and the bicone so your thread is exiting in the center **(FIGURE 15)**.

13 Add 1 C, 1 D, and 1 C. Pass through the fourth bead in the ring from right to left. Add 1 C and continue through the D exited at the beginning of this step, the new C, and the new D **(FIGURE 16)**.

14 Congratulations! You've made it this far and you're on the home stretch now. Exiting the fifth of the new D, add 1 C and pass through the fifth D in the ring. Add 1 C and pass through the first D added for the center. Add 1 C and pass through the fifth D added for the center. Then pass through the fifth D in the ring again **(FIGURE 17)**.

Now you're ready to pass your thread through to the other side of the ring and complete the top of the cherry in the same way.

15 Repeat steps 9 to 14, but before you add the last C of step 14, insert the knotted end of the cherry stem into the ring of 5 C. Pull tight and pass through these 5 C again.

16 Despite your best efforts to work with tight tension, no doubt your cherry is a little soft. Tighten it up, as follows: To make it firm, pass through the 5 C

in the center of each set of 5 bicones and pass through the first C again to tighten. Pass through the next D and into the next ring of 5 C and tighten it in the same way.

After passing through all the 5-bead centers, continue passing through the triangles formed by the D and C in a random pattern. Work until all the thread is used up and your cherry is very firm. Cut the thread near the beads.

If necessary to stiffen the cherry, dip it in Pledge with Future Finish Floor Polish and allow to dry on waxed paper.

Prepare the Chain

Carefully open a link at one end of the chain by twisting the sides of the link apart with 2 pairs of needle-nose pliers, as follows: Rotate 1 side away from you and 1 side toward you. Insert one side of the clasp. Close the link. Do the same with the other side of the clasp.

At the center of the chain, open a link, insert the split ring on one pair of cherries, and close the link. Open the link immediately next to this link and insert the split ring attached to a leaf. Close the link by reversing the way you opened it. Add another leaf on the other side of the cherries the same way. Move up the chain 1½ inches (4 cm) and add another pair of cherries with a leaf on each side. Repeat, then add the cherries on the other side of the center.

36

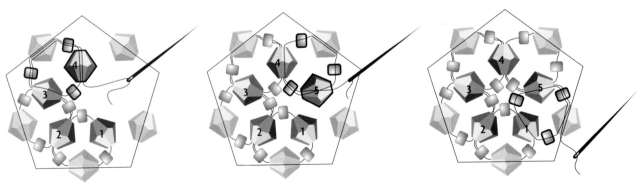

FIGURE 15   **FIGURE 16**   **FIGURE 17**

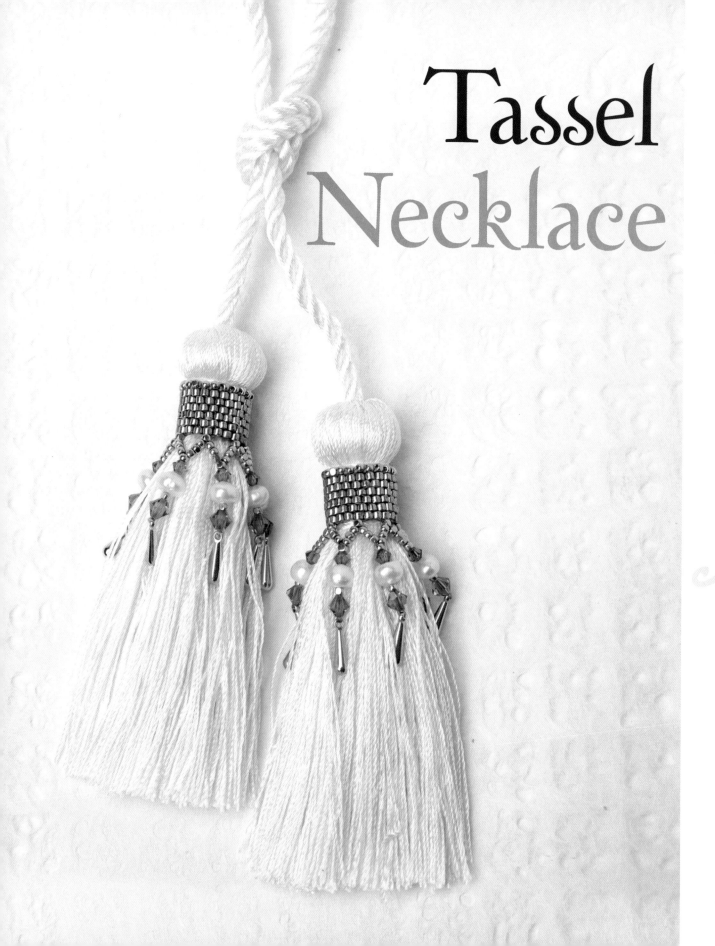

Tassel
Necklace

Tassel
Necklace

Beginners can create an elegant necklace while learning basic flat peyote stitch. A pair of purchased tassels on a rope is embellished with a peyote strip enhanced with a fringe.

SUPPLIES

Pair of 3-inch (7.5 cm) tassels on a 27-inch (68.5 cm) twisted rope*

A, size 11° cylinder beads, 3 g

B, size 15° seed beads, 2 g

16 pearls, 4 to 5 mm

16 bicone crystals, 3 mm

16 bicone crystals, 4 mm

16 small drop pendant charms

Nymo beading thread, size D

Scissors

Size 10 beading needle

*I suggest Wright's 183-9069-112, which is available in various colors.

Dimensions: *33 inches (84 cm) long*

1 Using cylinder beads, make a peyote strip 6 beads wide and 42 rows long as follows:

Row 1: Thread a needle with 2 yards (1.8 m) of thread, add a bead, and pass forward through this bead again to create a stopper bead. String on 6 A **(FIGURE 1)**.

Row 2: Add 1 A and, skipping 1 A, pass through the next A. Repeat 2 times **(FIGURE 2)**. Tie the working thread to the tail.

Rows 3–42: Repeat Row 2, working back and forth and adding 3 A per row.

FIGURE 1

FIGURE 2

counting rows in peyote stitch

In peyote stitch, for Row 1, the beginning row, you're actually adding the beads for the first two rows. For each additional row, which is offset from the previous row, 3 beads are added. Thus, when you count the rows along one lengthwise edge, count 1, 3, 5, 7, etc., and 2, 4, 6, 8, etc. along the other side. For this project you will end with Row 42 **(FIGURE 3)**.

FIGURE 3

2 Whip stitch 1 B to the thread, which connects the beads along one edge of the peyote strip **(FIGURE 4)**.

3 On the opposite edge, add the fringe as follows: With thread exiting an A on the bottom edge, pass the needle under the next thread between the next 2 A.

4 Add 4 B, one 3 mm crystal, 1 pearl, 1 B, one 4 mm crystal, and the pendant drop. Pass back through the crystal, 1 B, 1 pearl, 1 crystal, and 1 B. Add 3 B. Pass through the third connecting thread along the strip and back through the last B.*

5 Repeat from * to * along the edge **(FIGURE 5)**.

6 Place the peyote strip around the tassel about ½ inch (1.3 cm) from the top and weave the 2 ends of the peyote strip together **(FIGURE 6)**. Stitch the strip to the tassel.

7 Repeat all steps to make the second tassel.

FIGURE 4

FIGURE 5

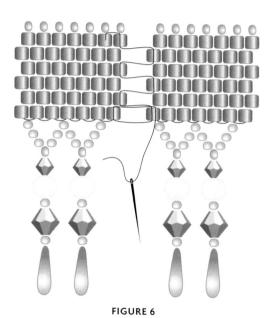

FIGURE 6

39

A delicate, lightweight, exquisite, and—best of all—easy to make necklace! Vary the beads at the tip of each branch for interesting effects. For example, you might add orange beads to resemble bittersweet.

Pussy Willow Necklace

SUPPLIES

About 100 small, oval pearls*

A, size 11° cylinder beads in 2 or 3 closely related colors, about 10 g

B, size 15° seed beads, 3 g

35 crystal bicones, 4 mm

Toggle clasp

Nylon beading thread, size D

Microcrystalline wax

Size 12 beading needle

Disposable lighter

Make sure the holes are large enough for 4 strands of thread; these are sometimes referred to as fat rice pearls.

Dimensions: 17¼ inches (44 cm) long

Branching Base

The necklace is constructed of peyote stitch branches, with each branch worked off the previous one.

1 Thread the beading needle with 3 yards (2.7 m) of thread. Bring the ends together, knot, clip the tails 1 mm from the knot, melt the knot, and wax the strands so that they adhere to each other. Pass the needle through the loop on half of the clasp so the knot is near the loop. Separate the strands of thread between the clasp and the knot. Pass the needle between the strands, creating a lark's head knot. Pull tight **(FIGURE 1)**.

2 Attach the clasp and beginning branch by stringing 8 A, 1 pearl, and 1 B **(FIGURE 2)**.

FIGURE 1

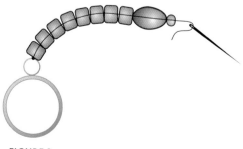

FIGURE 2

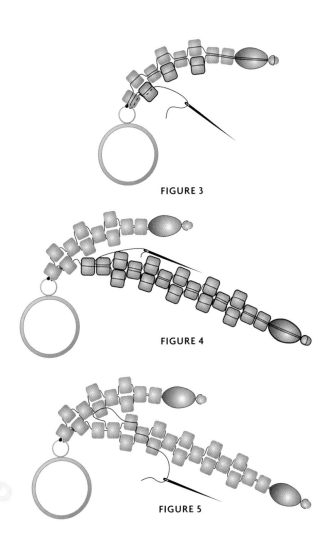

FIGURE 3

FIGURE 4

42

FIGURE 5

3 Pass back through the pearl and 2 A, then peyote stitch with A to the toggle clasp. Pass through the loop of the clasp. Turn and pass forward through 2 A **(FIGURE 3)**.

4 Add 13 A, 1 pearl, and 1 B, and, skipping the B, pass back through the pearl and 2 A. Do 5 peyote stitches with A back down the strand toward the previous branch **(FIGURE 4)**. End exiting the second bead strung of the 13 A.

5 To make the turn to begin a new branch, pass forward through a "sticking up" A in the previous branch as shown in **FIGURE 5** (the fourth bead of the first branch), then through the third, fourth, and fifth A in the new branch, so you're exiting a "sticking up" bead on the new branch on the side opposite the previous branch.

6 Begin a new branch by repeating steps 4 and 5. By turning this way, your thread doesn't show, the angle of the branch is smooth, and you reinforce the necklace.

If you wish, vary the length of the branches, but always use an odd number of A when beginning a new branch.

7 Work until the necklace measures 17 inches (43 cm) or the desired length, then add the second half of the clasp. Sew on flowers (see instructions on page 43).

Making the Branches Curve

Here's the secret: Wax the thread heavily and keep tight tension on the branch after the beads are strung by wrapping the working thread over your forefinger and holding it with your middle finger. Hold the branch curved on the pad of your forefinger, then add the new beads to the branch with soft tension, keeping the strand curved as you work.

adding new thread

When you have about 4 inches (10 cm) of thread left, leave the needle on the thread. Prepare a new thread as in the first step for this project. Bring the second needle through 3 or 4 beads so that it comes out of the same bead in the same direction as the previous thread. Tie the previous thread and the new thread together with a square knot. Apply clear nail polish to the knot. Thread the remaining end of the previous thread through several beads and clip.

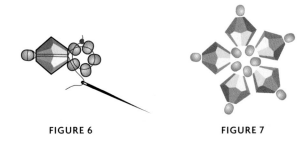

FIGURE 6   **FIGURE 7**

Inspired by bittersweet, the extra long necklace above is made with 3- and 4-mm round orange glass beads. Right: For a more sparkly necklace, use 75 to 100 4-mm bicone crystals instead of pearls. About 75 are needed for a 17-inch (43 cm) necklace. Adjust the quantity for a longer necklace.

43

Flowers

Bicone crystals add a touch of sparkle.

1 Prepare the thread as described in the first step. Add 5 B to form a ring. Use the lark's head knot method to join as described in step 1 to begin the necklace. Pass through the first B to the left of the knot **(FIGURE 6, BLUE LINE)**.

2 Add 1 bicone and 1 B and pass back through the bicone. Pass through the next B in the ring **(FIGURE 6, RED LINE)**.

3 Repeat step 2 four more times **(FIGURE 7)**. Sew the flower to a point where 2 branches meet near the center of the necklace. Knot the thread between beads and weave in the tail.

4 Make 6 more flowers. Sew them to the necklace as follows: The first flower is in the center of the necklace. Sew the remaining flowers each 2 inches (5 cm) apart.

Let your pendant inspire your necklace. For my very first Sea Moss Necklace, my pendant suggested watery depths and undersea life forms such as moss. In this necklace, the seed bead texture complements the smooth surface of a pendant with a pleasing contrast that doesn't overwhelm it.

SUPPLIES

Glass pendant

Size 6° or 8° seed beads for the backbone strand, about 15 g

11° seed beads in several colors related to your pendant, 35 to 45 g

Miscellaneous small beads up to 8 mm, stone chips, size 6° or 8° seed beads, rondelles, etc., 25 to 50 g

Multistrand clasp (3 or 4 holes)

2 yards (1.8 m) of nylon bead cord, size F

Nymo beading thread, size D

2 size 10 beading needles

Microcrystalline wax

Disposable lighter

2 pieces of foam board, 9 x 12 x ¼ inch (23 cm x 30.5 cm x 6 mm) and 6 x 12 x ¼ inch (15 cm x 30.5 cm x 6 mm)

White tacky glue

Straight pins

Transparent tape

Clear nail polish

Small box lid for scooping beads, approximately 4 x 4 x 1 inch (10 x 10 x 2.5 cm)

Cutting blade

Dimensions: *24¼ inches (61.5 cm) long*

Sea Moss Necklace

45

The Sea Moss Necklace begins with a "backbone" strand of beads that supports a glass pendant. The backbone strand is strung with size 6° or 8° seed beads that can accommodate a heavier cord, as well as several other strands of thread. (Stone beads aren't recommended because their holes are often small.) To this backbone strand, 3 or 4 rows of seed bead loops are added, then strands of seed beads are woven in and out, back and forth, through these loops. These strands may be accented with chips or larger beads. The piece is worked on a template to protect the glass pendant while working and to assure that the necklace maintains its curved shape when completed.

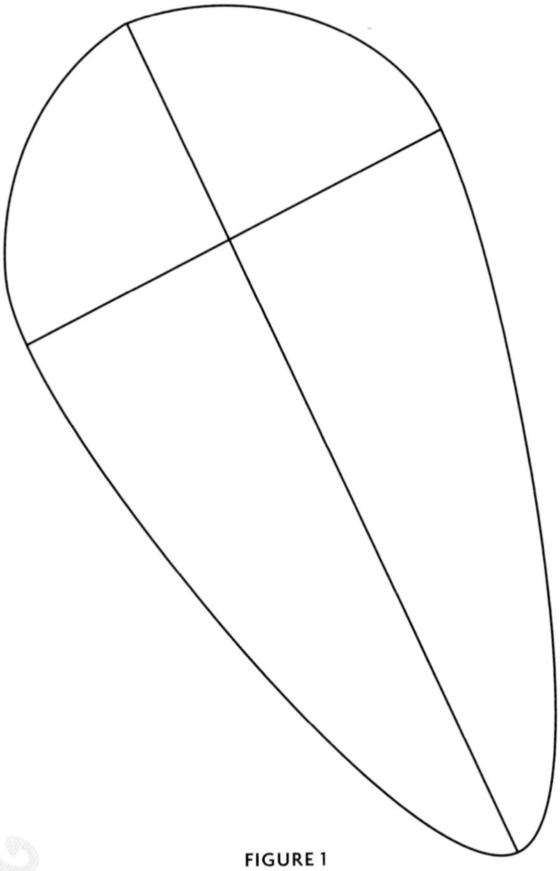

Make the Template

Using the 6 x 12-inch (15 x 30.5 cm) piece of foam board, draw and cut out the template shown using a cutting blade (you may photocopy this page; **FIGURE 1**). This template results in a necklace about 26 inches (66 cm) long. If desired, lengthen or shorten by cutting the template along the horizontal line and spreading it apart. For a necklace 2 inches (5 cm) longer, spread the template apart 1 inch (2.5 cm). Mark the center line. Glue the template to the second piece of foam board, centering it on the board 1½ inches (4 cm) from the top. Use tacky white glue for quick drying. This template may be reused for other necklaces.

String the Backbone Strand

1 Tape your pendant to the template, placing the stringing hole along the bottom pointed edge of the template. Use straight pins to position the clasp on the board at the top center line. Bring the 2 ends of the size F cord together and knot the ends together with an overhand knot **(FIGURE 2)**. The thread is used double. Clip the tail ¹⁄₁₆ inch (2 mm) from the knot and melt the knot by placing it near the base of the disposable lighter flame, but not in it. *Important:* Check to see that the knot is secure by pulling the strands apart.

2 Make a harness to guide the cord through the beads by stringing a beading needle with 6 inches (15 cm) of size D Nymo thread. Pass this strand through the loop of the bead cord and tie the thread ends together with a square knot **(FIGURE 3)**.

3 Anchor the cord to one half of the clasp using a lark's head or sales tag knot **(FIGURE 4)**. Pass the cord through 1 hole of the clasp nearest the template, then bring the other end through the loop just formed.

4 String on backbone beads to reach the pendant, pass through the pendant, and string more backbone beads to reach the other half of the clasp. Pass through the loop of the clasp nearest the template and back through the first bead. Tie a half-hitch knot around the thread and between the beads. Pass through 2 beads and knot again. Bring the thread through 3 more beads and clip. Apply clear nail polish to all knots.

46

FIGURE 1
Enlarge 200%

FIGURE 2

FIGURE 3

In a square knot, the left thread goes over the right and around it. Then the right thread goes over the left and passes through the loop.

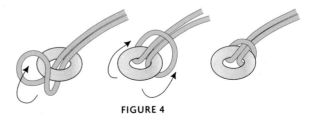

FIGURE 4

Loop Rows

To attach thread to the clasp, thread a beading needle with 3 to 4 yards (2.7 to 3.7 m) of Nymo thread and bring the ends together. (The thread is used double.) Wax it well so the strands stick together. This is important because it keeps the thread from tangling, the beads from slipping, and the thread from showing. Knot the ends together with an overhand knot. Clip the excess thread ¹⁄₁₆ inch (2 mm) from the knot and melt as described above. Attach the thread to the middle hole of the clasp using the sales tag knot **(FIGURE 4)**. Give it a firm tug to make sure it is secure!

String the Beads

1 Beads are strung with the scooping method. Place a generous amount of seed beads in the box lid and mound them up in one corner. Hold the needle between your thumb and middle finger and scoop beads from the dish with a slight upward motion (like an airplane taking off). Aim your needle for the middle of the pile where the needle is likely to catch a bead, not along the bottom where beads are likely to be lying with their holes vertical. You should be able to fill a 2-inch (5 cm) beading needle in 3 or 4 scoops.

2 String about 1½ inches (4 cm) of beads and pass through the fourth or fifth bead from the clasp. Continue around the backbone strand in this way until you have a series of loops formed. When you come to the pendant, pass the needle through it. Be careful here, though, to check the size of the hole in your pendant. If it's large and the seed beads might slip through, pass through the last backbone bead right before the pendant and the first one coming out of

the pendant hole. Continue stringing loops up to the clasp. Pass through the clasp and then back through 2 or 3 of the beads just strung, going in the opposite direction from the way you were just working. Now work around the necklace in the opposite direction **(FIGURE 5)**.

3 Make 2 or 3 more sets of loops in this way, going into a different backbone bead on each round, making smaller or larger loops as you wish and with the same or different color. A few silver-lined beads will add sparkle. Transparent beads will lighten the feel of the piece. As you string some loops you may wish to begin adding small beads, chips, or rondelles within the loop. These give fullness and texture to the necklace.

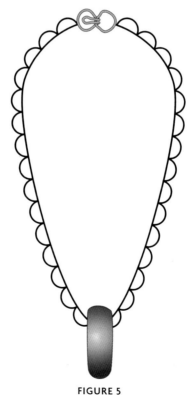

FIGURE 5

The clasp, the backbone strand of beads, the pendant, and one row of loops.

47

48

Intertwine

1 With 3 or 4 sets of loops in place, begin interweaving, as follows: Continue with the same thread. After passing through the clasp, pass through the last few beads strung, then string on a needleful of beads and push them all the way to the end of the thread near the necklace. Randomly weave the thread in and out of the loops, passing back and forth and up and down. If you only pass back and forth, laying round after round on top of each other, you'll end up with lines of color that meander snakelike across the top of your piece rather than an integrated, intertwined appearance. As you string, add a small bead or stone chip every few inches.

2 At the point where a needleful of beads ends, pass your needle through whichever bead your needle happens to be near to anchor the strand. String on more beads, weave in and out, up and down, and anchor again in the nearest bead. After completing 3 or 4 rounds this way, your necklace will begin to take on a mossy, ropelike appearance. Do as many rounds as you wish until you achieve the desired look and size. Be careful not to overpower your pendant, however. When you have 8 to 10 strands interwoven, tie off your thread just as you did with the end of the cord on the first strand of backbone beads.

3 A variety of looks can be achieved by the way your interweaving is done. Smaller loops in the beginning result in a tighter, narrower rope. Large loops result in a less dense, more open look.

adding new thread

After anchoring a needleful of beads and when you have about 4 inches (10 cm) of thread left, stop and leave the needle on the thread. Thread a second beading needle prepared as described above. Bring the second needle through the last 8 to 10 beads so that it comes out of the same bead in the same direction as the first thread. Tie the first thread and the second thread together with a square knot. Apply clear nail polish to the knot. Thread the remaining end of the first thread through nearby beads and clip the excess.

Fit for a queen, this regal necklace will make you consider getting a tiara to go with it. Beaded with triangle weave, it features 13 triangles made with bicone crystals and seed beads. Each triangle is made separately and then strung with a clasp at each end. Select a color that looks good on your skin, or make a longer necklace to wear over a blouse.

SUPPLIES

A, size 11° gold seed beads, 5 g* **

B, 261 purple velvet crystal bicones, 4 mm**

2 gold round metal beads, 3 mm

Lobster-claw clasp and closed ring

Scissors

Crystal Fireline braided beading thread, 6 lb.

Size 12 beading needle

Microcrystalline wax

Disposable lighter

*Charlottes or 1-cuts work well.

**For a 20-inch (51 cm) necklace, add 1 g of seed beads and 40 bicones.

Dimensions: 18 inches (46 cm) long

Majesty
Necklace

51

Each triangle is made separately and then strung.

Triangles

1 Thread the needle with 1½ yards (1.4 m) of thread. Bring the ends together. Wax well so that the strands adhere to each other like a single strand. Knot the ends together with an overhand knot. Clip the tails 1 mm from the knot and melt the tails slightly with the lighter. (Don't put the tails in the flame, just near it.) Test the knot by pulling on the strands to make sure it's secure.

2 In the diagrams that follow, the new beads and the new thread path are shown with a bold line. Make 13 triangles as follows: To begin, count out 1 pile of 19 bicones and 28 seed beads.

triangle weave rule

Working triangle beadwork is much like right angle weave. You can only pass your needle through the bead directly to the right or left of the bead your thread is exiting.

FIGURE 1

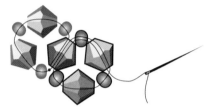

FIGURE 2

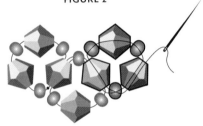

FIGURE 3

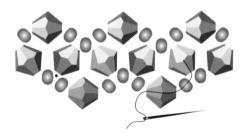

FIGURE 4

Row 1:

1 String 1 seed bead and 1 bicone 3 times.

2 Pass the beads to within 1 inch (2.5 cm) of the knot. Separate the threads between the beads and the knot. Pass the needle between the threads. Pull tight to form a ring. Pass back through the last bicone strung **(FIGURE 1)**.

3 Add 1 seed bead and 1 bicone twice, plus 1 seed bead. Pass through the bicone your thread exited at the beginning of this step from the opposite end **(FIGURE 2)**.

4 Continue through the next seed bead and the next bicone **(FIGURE 2)**.

5 Add 1 seed bead and 1 bicone twice, plus 1 seed bead. Pass through the bicone your thread exited at the beginning of this step from the opposite end. Continue through the next seed bead and bicone to the right **(FIGURE 3)**.

6 Repeat steps 3 to 5 once more. Your piece should now look like **FIGURE 4**. Lay it out in front of you so that the knot is on the lower left. Note that there are 3 bicones sitting horizontally across the top and 2 bicones sitting horizontally across the bottom of the strip. Between

these horizontal rows of bicones are 6 bicones sitting diagonally. The needle should be exiting the bicone on the lower right.

7 Pass the thread through 1 seed bead, the second bicone from the right, and then left through the next bicone **(FIGURE 4)**.

Row 2:

1 Add 1 seed bead and 1 bicone twice, then add 1 more seed bead. Pass through the bicone your thread exited going from right to left, then continue through the next seed bead and the next bicone **(FIGURE 5)**.

2 Add 1 seed bead and 1 bicone twice, plus 1 seed bead. Pass through the bicone your thread exited at the beginning of this step, then continue through all the new beads added in this step except the last seed bead. Add 1 seed bead, then pass through the bicone to the left from right to left **(FIGURE 6)**.

3 Add 1 seed bead, 1 bicone, and 1 seed bead. Pass through the next bicone to the right. Continue through the next seed bead, bicone, seed bead, and the bottom bicone that's sitting horizontally **(FIGURE 7)**.

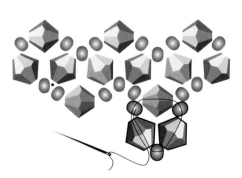

FIGURE 5

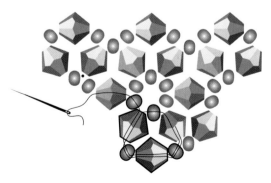

FIGURE 6

Row 3:

1 Add 1 seed bead and 1 bicone twice, plus 1 seed bead. Pass back through the last bicone.

2 Add 1 seed bead, 1 bicone, and 1 seed bead. Pass through the bicone your thread exited at the beginning of this step (**FIGURE 8**). Weave in the thread and clip it.

Join the Triangles

1 Prepare the thread as described in the very first step of these instructions. Pass the needle through one half of the clasp and push the clasp to within 1 inch (2.5 cm) of the knot. Separate the strands between the knot and the clasp, and pass the needle between the strands.

2 Add one 3 mm round metal bead. Push it toward the clasp so it covers the knot.

3 Add 1 bicone and 1 seed bead. Pass through the 3 bicones and 8 seed beads across the top of the triangle (**FIGURE 9**).

4 Add the remaining triangles as follows: Add 1 seed bead, 1 bicone, and 1 seed bead, and pass through the beads across the top of the next triangle. Repeat for the remaining triangles.

5 Add 1 seed bead, 1 bicone, the 3 mm round bead, and the other half of the clasp. Pass back through the 3 mm bead. Knot the thread between the beads with a half-hitch knot. Pass through the next bead and knot again. Weave in the tail and clip (**FIGURE 10**).

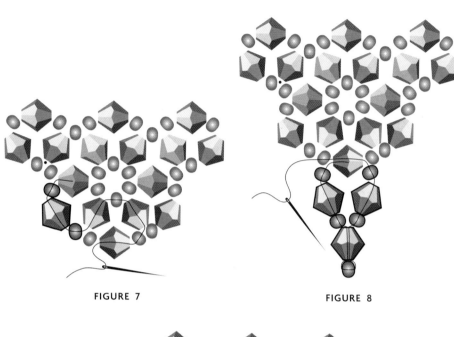

FIGURE 7

FIGURE 8

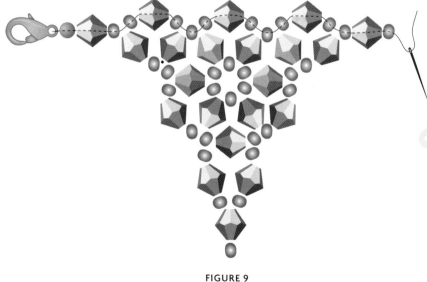

FIGURE 9

FIGURE 10

54

Fortune-Teller
Beads

Fortune-Teller Beads

The inner glow of the beaded resin beads reminds me of a fortune-teller's crystal ball. The tiny crystals in the netting shimmer as the light passes through them. To make one, you'll bead a strip of netting with picots on both sides, join the ends, gather the bottom edge, slip in a resin bead, gather the top edge, and presto—a beaded bead!

SUPPLIES

FOR EACH BEADED BEAD:

1 orange round resin bead, 19 mm

A, 24 size 11° gold round seed beads

B, size 15° rose topaz 3-cut seed beads, 2 g

C, 48 crystal jonquil bicones, 2.5 mm

Fireline beading thread, 6 lb.

Microcrystalline wax

Size 12 beading needles

Scissors

FOR THE NECKLACE:

2 gold round metal beads, 3 mm

20 gold round metal beads, 5 mm

1 gold lobster-claw clasp with soldered ring

18 inches (46 cm) of beading wire

2 gold crimp tubes

Crimping pliers

Make 17, or the desired amount.

Dimensions: *16¾ inches (42.5 cm) long*

In each illustration, the new thread and beads are shown with a bold outline.

1 Thread a needle with 1½ yards (1.4 m) of thread, and wax it well so that the strands adhere to each other like a single strand. String 1 A, leaving a 4-inch (10 cm) tail. Pass through the bead again, making a stopper bead **(FIGURE 1)**. This bead will be removed later.

2 Add 1 C and 3 B, 3 times. Add 1 B. Pass back through the last 3 B and the next C. These beads form a picot **(FIGURE 2)**.

FIGURE 1

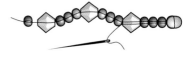

FIGURE 2

3 Add 3 B, 1 C, and 3 B. Pass through the first crystal added in the previous row (scallop made). Your thread should now be exiting the C before the stopper bead. Remove the stopper bead and tie the working thread to the tail with a square knot **(FIGURE 3)**.

4 Add 3 B, 1 C, 3 B, and 1 A. Pass back through the first 3 B and the C, making a picot **(FIGURE 4)**.

5 Add 3 B, 1 C, and 3 B. Pass forward through the next crystal in the previous row **(FIGURE 5)**.

6 Add 3 B, 1 C, 3 B, and 1 A. Pass back through the 3 B and the C **(FIGURE 6)**.

FIGURE 3

FIGURE 4

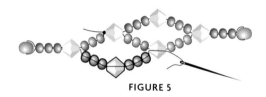

FIGURE 5

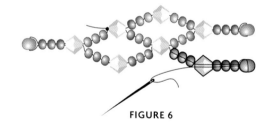

FIGURE 6

57

7 Repeat steps 3 through 6 until there are 12 picots on one side and 11 on the other side and you have just completed a picot on the side opposite the knot (FIGURE 7).

8 Lace up the ends to form a tube, as follows: Hold the ending edge and the beginning edge so they're almost next to each other. Add 3 B. Pass through the C on the opposite end of the beadwork. Repeat this step once more. Add 3 B, 1 C, 3 B, and 1 A. Pass back through the 3 B and the C. Add 3 B. Tie the working thread to the tail with a square knot (FIGURE 8).

9 Pass through the beads to the opposite side so that the thread is exiting a bead on the tip of the picot. Pass through all the tip beads on that side. Pull the thread tight so that the tip beads are touching and the piece forms a cup. Pass through all the tip beads 2 more times. Knot the thread between the beads.

10 Pass through to the other side of the strip and pass through all the tip beads. Place the resin bead in the cup just formed, with the hole aligned with the hole in the bottom of the cup. Pull the thread tight to close the cup. Pass through all the tip beads 2 more times. Knot the thread and weave in the tails.

11 Repeat steps 1 through 10 to make a total of 17 beaded beads, or the desired amount.

12 To assemble the necklace, string the end of the beading wire through a crimp tube, one half of the clasp, and back through the crimp tube, then flatten the tube using the crimping pliers. String one 3 mm gold bead and two 5 mm gold beads. Add 1 beaded bead and one 5 mm gold bead 17 times. Add one 5 mm gold bead, one 3 mm gold bead, 1 crimp tube, and the other half of the clasp. Pass back through the crimp tube and 3 or 4 beads. Flatten the crimp tube and trim the beading wire.

Adjustments

Resin beads vary in size, so you may need to make some adjustments. For a smaller or larger interior bead, increase or decrease the number of beads in the picot, the number of beads between the crystals, or the number of picots on each side. After adjusting, continue from step 8.

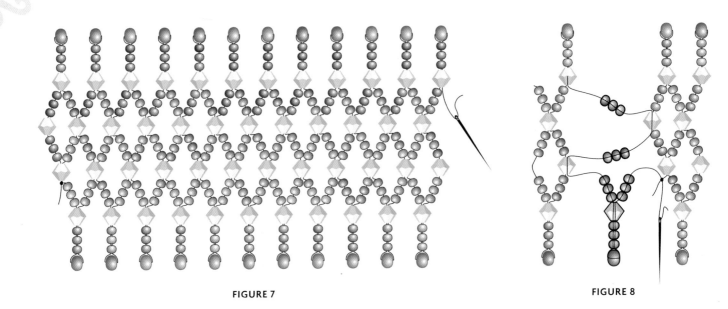

FIGURE 7   **FIGURE 8**

Flatter your face with the softness of a silk flower framed with the sparkle of crystals. Learn to make a silk flower and a neck ring with crystals and cylinder beads.

Apple Blossom Necklace

SUPPLIES

FOR THE NETTED CRYSTAL TUBE:

720 crystal bicones, 4 mm

Size 11° metallic cylinder beads, 9 g

24 inches (61 cm) of waxed cotton cord, 2 mm diameter

2 fold-over end covers

1 lobster-claw clasp and closed ring

2 jump rings

Fireline braided beading thread, 6 lb.

2 size 10 beading needles

Microcrystalline wax

Lighter

Flat-nose pliers

Scissors

FOR THE FLOWER:

¾ yard (68.5 cm) of 1½-inch (4 cm) wide ribbon with double-wired edge

40 crystal bicones for flower center and embellishment, 4 mm

16 crystal bicones for rope embellishment, 6 mm

Size 15° seed beads, 1 g

Scissors

Dimensions: *18 inches (45.5 cm) long*

Prepare the Cotton Cord

The netted tube is worked over the cotton cord. Attach the fold-over end cover to the cotton cord. Fold one side over the cord and squeeze it with pliers, then fold the second side over and squeeze it with pliers.

Prepare the Thread

1 Thread a needle with 3 yards (2.7 m) of thread, bring the ends together, wax well so that the strands adhere to each other like a single strand, and knot the ends together with an overhand knot. (Thread is used double throughout because crystals can be sharp!) Clip the tails 1 mm from the knot and melt them slightly with a lighter. (Don't put the tails in the flame, just near it.) Test the knot by pulling on the strands to make sure it's secure.

FIGURE 1

2 String on 6 cylinder beads. Push the beads to within 1 inch (2.5 cm) of the knot. Separate the strands between the beads and the knot. Pass the needle between the strands, then pass back through the last cylinder bead added **(FIGURE 1)**. Insert the cord into the ring of beads. Pull the thread tight. Pass through the loop on the end of the fold-over end cover and, working clockwise (lefties should work counterclockwise), continue forward through one of the cylinder beads **(FIGURE 2)**.

FIGURE 2

61

DIANE FITZGERALD'S FAVORITE BEADING PROJECTS

3 Add 1 bicone and 2 cylinder beads. Pass through the second cylinder bead, counting from where your thread exits a bead **(FIGURE 3)**. Repeat this step two more times **(FIGURES 4 AND 5)**.

4 Add 1 bicone and 2 cylinder beads and pass through the first cylinder bead after the next bicone for desired length.

5 Determine your desired length, usually about 18 inches (45 cm) minus about ¾ inch (2 cm) for the clasp. Cut the cotton cord to this length. Add the fold-over end cover to the second end.

End the Tube

1 Continue adding beads until you've covered the cotton cord and the second end cover.

2 Add 1 cylinder bead and pass through the first cylinder bead after the next bicone 3 times. Pull tight. Pass through these 3 cylinder beads again and pass through the loop of the end cover, then through a cylinder bead. Knot between the beads twice and pass through several beads. Clip the tails. Attach the lobster-claw clasp to one end and the closed ring to the other end with jump rings.

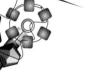

FIGURE 3

FIGURE 4

FIGURE 5

FIGURE 6

Make the Flower

1 Draw the wire on one side of the ribbon to form a gather. This gathered edge will form the bottom of the flower. Draw halfway on one end, then halfway on the other end.

2 With 1 yd (91.5 cm) of thread in your needle and the end knotted, bring the right side of the ends of the ribbon together and sew a seam ⅛ inch (3 mm) from the edge with a running stitch. Leave the wires on the top edge and bottom edge sticking out a little for now. Fold the seam to the inside and sew a second seam to enclose the raw edge. (This is called a French seam, a seam that encloses the seam allowance on the inside of a sewn item.)

3 Continue to draw the wire tight along the bottom, forming a tight gather. Twist the ends together tightly and tuck under the flower. On the top edge, pull out the wires slightly, twist together, and tuck to the wrong side.

4 Fold the gathered ribbon in half with the seam at one end. Sew along the gathered edge to join the two halves using the overcasting stitch (see box). Sew the flower to the crystal rope. Sew 4 mm bicone crystals to the center of the flower and a few near the flower on the rope. Add the 6 mm bicone crystals near the flower along the rope. Sew these on like adding fringe as follows: with thread anchored in the flower (or on the rope), add a bicone and a size 15° seed bead and pass back through the bicone. Pass through the ribbon (or beads) to the next place where you will add a bicone **(FIGURE 6)**.

overcast stitch

Also known as whip stitch, the overcast stitch is usually used to join two edges. With thread anchored in the fabric and holding the two edges aligned, pass the needle through both edges. Repeat for desired length.

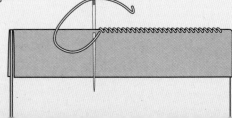

This lovely little basket may be filled with tiny glass flowers and beaded leaves and worn either as a pin or as a pendant on a chain. You'll learn an unusual Zulu stitch that creates vertical ridges connected with horizontal beads. Square stitch is used for the handle.

SUPPLIES

A, light brown size 11° Japanese seed beads, 7 g

B, dark brown size 11° Japanese seed beads, 7 g

Small amounts of green seed beads or cylinder beads for the leaves

Pressed glass flower beads or buttons or margaritas

Size 10 or 12 beading needles

Nymo beading thread, size D

Pin back, 1¼ inches (3 cm) long, or chain for making a pendant

Microcrystalline wax

Scissors

Clear nail polish

Disposable lighter

Dimensions: *2½ inches (6.5 cm) tall*

May Basket

The basket flares out at the top with 8 spokes or vertical ridges and a handle at the top. Glass flower beads or buttons can be used to embellish the basket. The basket may be worked in 1 or 2 colors following the colors in the illustrations. After you've made 1, try a miniature version using size 15° beads.

Squares and Bridge Beads

The basket is worked from bottom to top. In these directions, the spokes are formed by adding 4 beads to each spoke on every row. These beads are shown in light brown in the illustrations. Squares sit on top of previous squares to form the basket's spokes (or ribs) and are connected to the previous square with bridge beads. Be careful—the thread in the squares may twist. If it does, the rib on the outside of the basket will be distorted. Bridge beads connect the squares. They're shown in dark brown in the illustrations (**SEE FIGURE 5**).

Row 1: Thread the needle with 2 yards (1.8 m) of thread, bring the ends together, wax well so that the strands adhere to each other like a single strand, and knot the ends together with an overhand knot. (Thread is used double throughout to give firmness to the basket.) Clip the tails 1 mm from the knot and melt the tails slightly with a lighter. (Don't put the tails in the flame, just near it.) Test the knot by pulling on the strands to make sure it's secure.

String on 8 A and push them to within 1 inch (2.5 cm) of the knot. Separate the strands between the beads and the knot and pass the needle between the strands **(FIGURE 1)**. Reverse direction and pass back through 1 A bead **(FIGURE 2)**. *Caution:* Do not let the knot slip into the bead.

Row 2: Work counterclockwise and keep the tension tight. *Add 4 A after each bead on the ring for a total of 8 sets of 4 beads. Arrange the 4 A beads so that they lie in 2 columns, forming a square **(FIGURE 3)*** Repeat from * to * 7 more times. After passing through the last bead in the beginning ring, pass up through the first 2 beads of the first square. See the arrow at **FIGURE 4**.

Row 3: Add 4 A. Pass the thread under the thread between the second and third beads of the square from the underside toward the center. Add 1 B. Pass through the corner bead (the second bead added for the set of 4 A) of the next square of 4 A beads **(FIGURE 5)**.

Repeat this step 7 more times. At the end of the row, pass through the next corner bead of the previous row, then up through the first 2 beads of the square above (3 beads total, a step up).

Rows 4 and 5: Repeat Row 3, except add 2 B instead of 1 B between the squares. Hold your piece so that it begins to form a cup rather than flattening out. Make sure you're passing your needle from the outside of the basket toward the center.

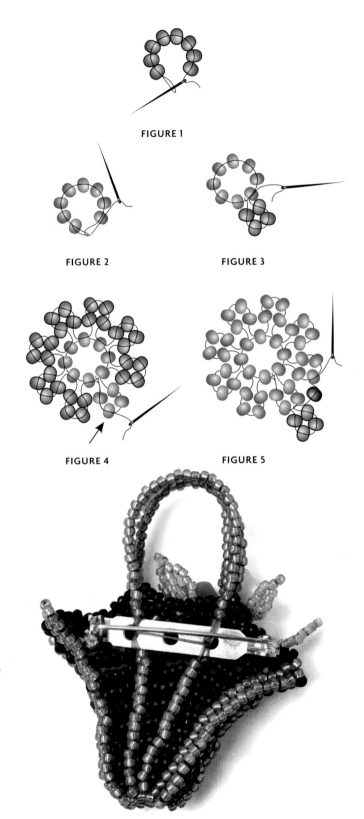

FIGURE 1

FIGURE 2

FIGURE 3

FIGURE 4

FIGURE 5

Row 6: Continue to add squares but add 3 B between each square 3 times, and 2 B before the next square.

Repeat this step once more. (The places where 2 B are added form the sides of the basket, and where 3 B are added, these will make the front and back flare out.)

Row 7: Repeat Row 6, being careful to place the 3 B above the previous 3 B and the 2 B above the 2 B to continue to form the sides and front and back of the basket.

Row 8: Repeat Row 6, adding 4 B above the 3 B and 2 B above the 2 B.

Row 9: Repeat Row 6, adding 5 B above the 4 B and 2 B above the 2 B.

Row 10: Repeat Row 6, adding 6 B above the 5 B and 2 B above the 2 B.

Row 11: Repeat Row 6, adding 7 B above the 6 B and 2 B above the 2 B.

Row 12: Form the scallops along the top of the basket, as follows: Continue to add the 4 bead squares with A to extend each of the spokes all around. Above the 7 B, add 5 A. Pass through the center bead of the 7 B in the row below. Add 5 A. Pass through the corner bead. Add only 2 bridge beads between the spokes along the sides, but do not add squares.

Row 13: Your thread should now be exiting a corner bead after adding 2 side beads. Pass down through the bead next to the corner bead. Add 3 A, then pass through the center bead of the first 5 A of the previous row. Add 3 A and pass through the center

bead of the second set of 5 A. Add 3 A beads and pass through the corner bead. For this row, extend the spines only on the 2 center spokes, both front and back. At the corners, after coming up through the corner bead, pass down through the bead next to it.

Add the 2 A for the side, then repeat this step once to complete the second side **(FIGURE 6)**. Knot between 2 beads and pass your needle through to 1 of the 2 middle spines to begin the handle.

Add the Handle

The handle is made with square stitch and appears as a continuation of the front spokes. Pass the thread through the beads so it is exiting upward through the 2 right beads at the top of one of the center front spokes. Add 4 A. Pass down through the 2 left beads of the spine, then up through the 2 right beads and the 2 just added on the right **(FIGURES 7 AND 8)**.

Repeat this step for 2 inches (5 cm) and attach it to the other front spine on the same side of the basket **(FIGURE 9)**.

Make a second handle and attach it to the spokes on the back side. Sew the 2 handles together by linking a few beads across the top.
Note: The handles may also be attached front to back instead of front to front and back to back.

FIGURE 6

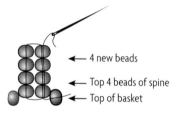

← 4 new beads
← Top 4 beads of spine
← Top of basket

FIGURE 7

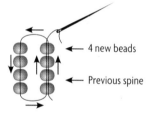

← 4 new beads
← Previous spine

FIGURE 8

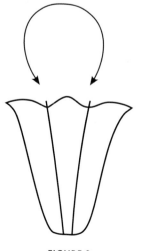

FIGURE 9

67

Attach Leaves and Flowers

Anchor thread in the top rim of the basket. Sew flower beads, buttons, or other embellishments on the edge of the basket, and make leaves along the edge of the basket between the flowers.

Leaves: String on 8 green seed beads. Pass back through the second-to-last seed bead. Add 5 seed beads. Pass through the first seed bead of the first 8, going toward the basket rim **(FIGURE 10)**. Pass through a bead in the rim of the basket and pass thread to the position where you wish to add another flower or leaf.

Sew a pin back to one side of the basket if you wish to use it as a pin. If you wish to use the basket as either a pin or pendant, sew on a pin back with a bail attached or pass the chain through the basket handles to wear it.

FIGURE 10

adding new thread

When you have about 4 inches (10 cm) of thread left, leave the needle on the thread. Thread a second needle, wax well, and knot the ends together with an overhand knot. Clip the tails 1 mm from the knot and melt them with a disposable lighter. Bring the second needle through 3 or 4 beads so that it exits the same bead in the same direction as the first thread. Tie the first thread and the second thread together with a square knot. Apply clear nail polish to the knot. Thread the remaining end of the first thread through several beads and clip the excess.

This bracelet with an open filigree look is sure to generate compliments. Enjoy it sparkling on your wrist whether you're working at the computer or out on the town.

Lacy Bracelet

SUPPLIES

A, 180 crystal bicones, 4 mm*

B, 600 crystal rounds, 2 mm**

2 crystal margaritas, 10 mm***

2 head pins, ¾ inch (2 cm) long

Fireline braided beading thread, 6 lb.

2 size 12 beading needles

Microcrystalline wax

Round-nose pliers

Scissors

Disposable lighter

Clear nail polish

*May substitute 180 firepolish round beads, 4 mm

**May substitute size 11° seed beads, 10 g

***May substitute 2 shank buttons, ¾ inch (2 cm) in diameter

Dimensions: *7½ inches (19 cm) long Length may vary depending on the beads used and your tension.*

The bracelet begins with the closure loops. With 3 yards (2.8 m) of thread in the needle, bring the ends together and wax well so that the strands adhere to each other like a single strand. The thread is used double.

Row 1: Make the closure loops and add the first set of 4 A as follows **(FIGURE 1)**: String 15 B and 1 A. Tie the beads in a ring. Pass back through the A and the next 4 B.

Add 4 B and 4 A. Pass forward through the first A.

Add 8 B, 1 A, and 11 B. Pass forward through the 4 B before the A.

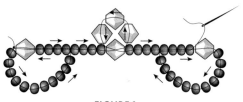

FIGURE 1

definitions

Pass through: Go forward in the same direction as the last pass; the same general direction as previously.

Pass back through: Go through the specified beads in the opposite direction of the last pass.

Row 2: Add the second and third sets of 4 A as follows **(FIGURE 2)**:
Add 6 B and 4 A. Pass forward through the first A again.
Add 2 B. Pass through the third A added in the previous row.
Add 2 B and 4 A. Pass forward through the first A again.
Add 6 B. Pass back through the first A added in the first row.

Row 3: Add the fourth, fifth, and sixth sets of 4 A as follows **(FIGURE 3)**: Add 12 B and 4 A. Pass forward through the first A again.
Add 2 B. Pass through the third A in the last set of 4 A in the previous row.
Add 2 B and 4 A. Pass through the first A again. Add 2 B. Pass through the third A added in the first set of 4 A in the previous row.
Add 2 B and 4 A. Pass through the first A again.

Make the Turn

Add 12 B. Pass back through the A in the second loop of Row 1. Then pass through the 6 B upward and the second B in the last set of 4 B added in the previous row **(FIGURE 4)**.

Continue through the 2 B and the first, second, and third A of the set of 4 A exited at the beginning of the turn.

Row 4: Add the seventh and eighth sets of 4 A as follows **(FIGURE 5)**:
Add 2 B and 4 A. Pass through the first of the 4 A again.
Add 2 B. Pass through the third A of the middle set of 4 A in the previous row.
Add 2 B and 4 A. Pass forward through the first A of this set of 4 A. Add 2 B. Pass through the third A of the next set of 4 A in the previous row.

Row 5: Make a figure eight in the center as follows **(FIGURE 6)**: Add 12 B and 4 A. Pass through the first of the 4 A again.
Add 6 B. Pass through the third A of the second set of 4 A in the previous row.
Add 2 B, 3 A, 2 B, and 4 A. Pass through the first A of the set of 4 A just added. Add 2 B. Pass through the third A of the first set of 3 A added in this step. Add 1 A. Pass through the first A added in this step.
Add 2 B. Pass through the third A of the first set of 4 A in the previous row.
Add 6 B and 4 A. Pass through the first A of these 4 A again.

72

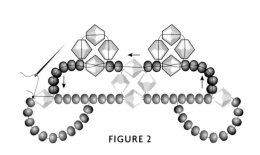

FIGURE 2

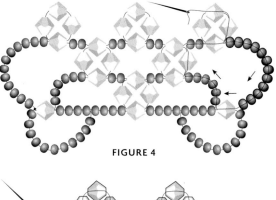

FIGURE 4

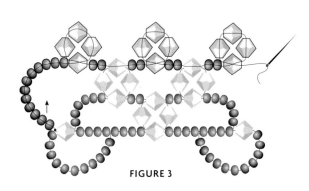

FIGURE 3

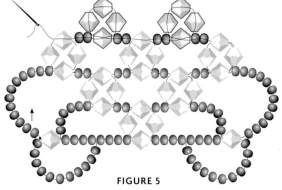

FIGURE 5

Make the Turn

Add 12 B. Pass back through the third A in the nearest loop of the row with 3 sets of 4 A (Row 3). Continue through the 2 B and the second A of the set of 4 A in the previous row. Continue through the 6 B. Pass through the first, second, and third A in the set of 4 A exited at the beginning of this step **(FIGURE 7)**.

Row 6: Add 6 B and 4 A. Pass through the first A again **(FIGURE 8)**.
  Add 2 B. Pass through the top A of the center column. Add 2 B and 4 A. Pass through the first A again.
  Add 6 B. Pass through the third A of the first set of 4 A added in the previous row.

Rows 7–14: Repeat Rows 3–6 twice.

Rows 15–16: Repeat Rows 3–4.

Row 17: Add 12 B, 1 A, and 6 B. Pass through the third (top) bead of the last set of 4 A added **(FIGURE 9)**.
  Add 2 B and 4 A. Pass through the first A again.
  Add 2 B. Pass through the third (top) A and second (side) A of the next set of 4 A. Pass through the next 6 B and the next A to the right.

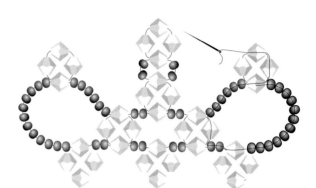

FIGURE 7

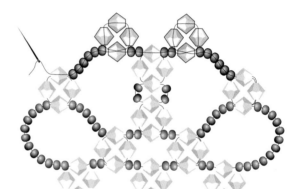

FIGURE 8

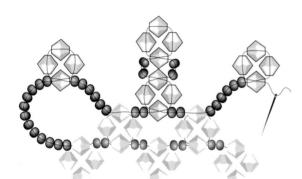

FIGURE 6

FIGURE 9

adding new thread

When you have about 4 inches (10 cm) of thread left, leave the needle on the thread. Thread a second needle, bring the ends together, and knot the ends together with an overhand knot. Clip the tails 1 mm from the knot and melt with a disposable lighter. Bring the second needle through 3 or 4 beads so that it exits the same bead in the same direction as the first thread. Tie the first thread and the second thread together with a square knot. Apply clear nail polish to the knot. Thread the remaining end of the first thread through several beads and clip the excess.

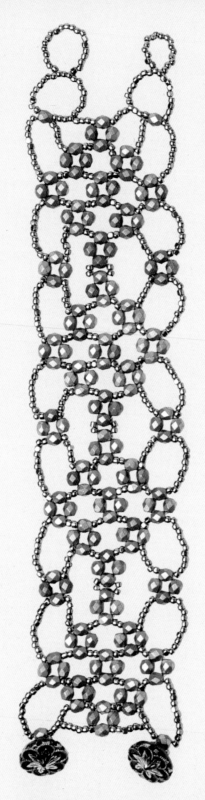

Turn

Add 12 B, 1 A, and 6 B. Pass through the third (top) A of the set of 4 A to the left. Continue through 2 B and up through the second A and the top A of the top center set of 4 A.

Row 18: This is the last row, where you'll add buttons **(FIGURE 10)**. Exiting the top center A going to the left; add 8 B. Pass through the single A added in the previous row.

Add 4 B, 1 button, and 4 B. Pass through the 4 B to the right and the center top A of the set of 4 A in the center.

Add 8 B. Pass through the single A in the loop on the left.

Add 4 B, 1 button, and 4 B. Pass back through the fourth bead to the right of the top center A. Knot the thread and weave in the tails at the beginning and end of the bracelet.

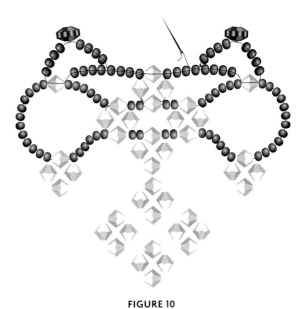

FIGURE 10

adjust length

To lengthen, when adding the buttons or when making loops at the beginning of the bracelet, add extra loops of beads as shown. To shorten, replace the A beads in Row 17 with buttons.

form the button

String a margarita onto a head pin. Clip the head pin ⅜ inch (1 cm) from the margarita and bend a simple loop with the round-nose pliers to form a shank button. Repeat for the other margarita and head pin.

Midnight Snowflakes

Midnight Snowflakes

Midnight Snowflakes is a shimmery necklace of crystal snowflakes hanging from a strand of cool bicones. Make a pair of snowflakes for earrings, or link a number of them for a bracelet or necklace.

SUPPLIES

A, 290 fuchsia AB crystal bicones, 3 mm

B, 90 fuchsia 2XAB crystal bicones, 4 mm

C, 10 fuchsia AB size 11° seed beads

Crystal Fireline braided beading thread, 6 lb.

24 inches (61 cm) of beading wire

Microcrystalline wax

2 gold crimp tubes

1 small gold filigree clasp

Size 12 beading needles

Scissors

Disposable lighter

Crimping pliers

Dimensions: 1 ¼ x 15¾ inches (3 x 40 cm)

Note: Each snowflake requires 48 bicone crystals. Snowflakes may be made with 3, 4, or 5 mm bicone crystals or a combination of sizes.

Snowflakes

Beads are added around the beginning ring in a counterclockwise fashion. "Pass forward" means to continue in the same direction. Each snowflake is made separately, then strung.

1 With 1 yard (91.5 cm) of thread in your needle, bring the ends together, wax well so that the strands adhere to each other like a single strand, and knot the ends together with an overhand knot. Clip the tails 1 mm from the knot and melt the ends with a lighter. (Don't put the tails in the flame, just near it.) Test the knot by pulling on the strands to make sure it's secure.

String 6 A and push them to within 1 inch (2.5 cm) of the knot. Separate the strands between the beads and the knot and pass the needle between the strands. Pull tight and pass back through the last bead strung, which is bead #6 **(FIGURE 1)**.

2 Add 5 A and pass forward through the bead exited in the first hexagon, bead #6, and then through bead #5 **(FIGURE 2)**.

3 Add 4 A (#12 to #15). Continue through bead #7, #5, and #4 **(FIGURE 3)**.

FIGURE 1

FIGURE 2

FIGURE 3

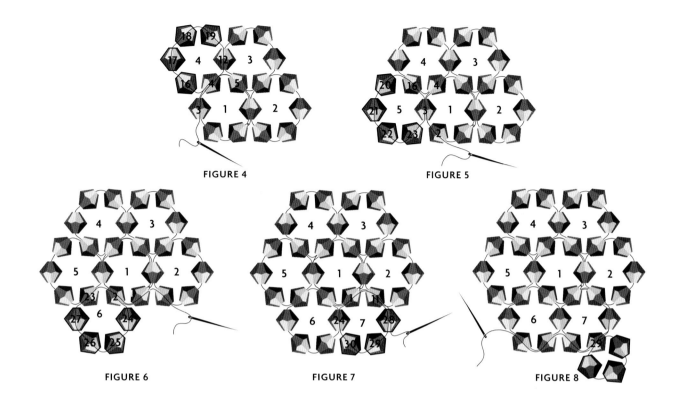

FIGURE 4

FIGURE 5

FIGURE 6

FIGURE 7

FIGURE 8

4 Add 4 A (#16 to #19). Pass forward through bead #12, #4, and #3 **(FIGURE 4)**.

5 Add 4 A (#20 to #23) and pass through #16 and #3 **(FIGURE 5)**. Continue through bead #2.

6 Add 4 A (#24 to #27) and pass through #23, #2, #5, #1, and #11 **(FIGURE 6)**.

7 Add 3 A (#28 to #30). Pass through #24, #1, #11, and #28 **(FIGURE 7)**.

8 Add the snowflake tips: Continue forward through #29. Add 3 B. Pass forward through the edge bicone just exited again. Continue to the center bead of the next set of 3 bicones along the edge (the next corner point of the hexagon), and add a tip of 3 B. Pass through the edge beads and add sets of 3 B to each of the next 4 corners **(FIGURE 8)**.

9 Follow all steps to make a total of 5 snowflakes.

String the Necklace

Beginning at one half of the clasp with 24 inches (61 cm) of beading wire and a crimp bead and a crimp bead, pass back through the crimp bead and flatten it with the crimping tool or needle-nose pliers. Add 50 A, 1 C, 1 snowflake, and 1 C. Add 10 A, 1 C, 1 snowflake, and 1 C, 4 times, then 50 A, a crimp, and the other half of the clasp. Pass back through the crimp, squeeze the crimp flat, and trim the beading wire.

earrings and pendants

For earrings or a pendant, add an optional ring on the sixth corner, as follows: Add 2 bicones and the ring. Pass back through the last bicone. Add 1 bicone. Pass through the corner bicone again. Knot the thread and weave in the tail **(FIGURE 9)**.

FIGURE 9

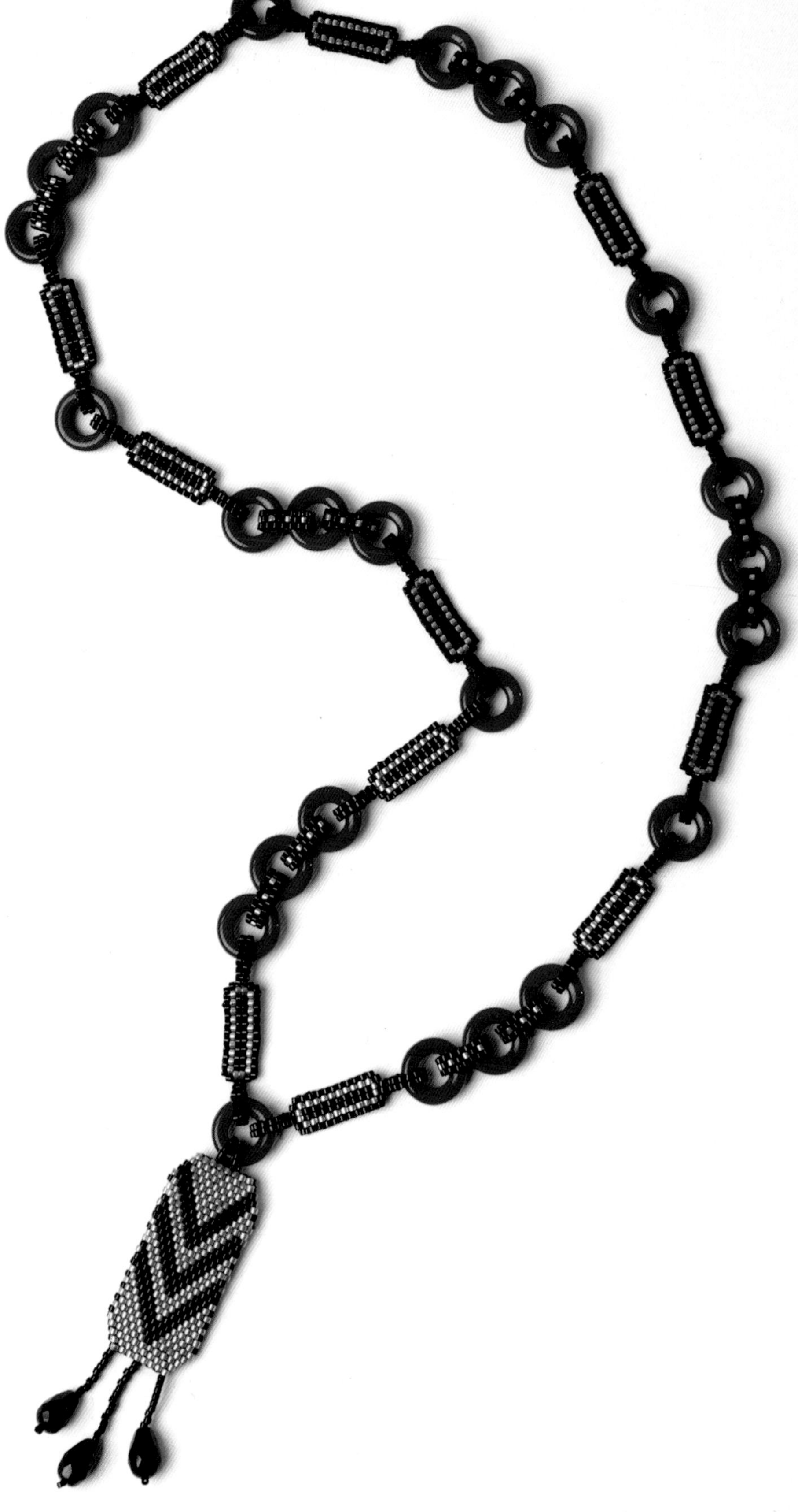

Re-create the excitement of the Roaring Twenties, when flappers wore long slender necklaces over straight chemise dresses and danced the Charleston into the wee hours of the morning. A combination of brick and peyote stitches joins the rings with two different types of links. The pendant is accented with bold V-shaped lines and drop-shaped bead dangles. This necklace slips over your head without a clasp. It's a show-stopper that's easy to make and sure to win compliments!

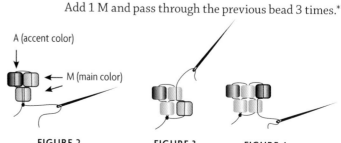

Art Deco Necklace

SUPPLIES

24 glass rings, 14 mm

M (main color), silver cylinder beads, 13 g

A (accent color), black cylinder beads, 4 g

3 firepolish drop beads, about 6 x 9 mm

Size 12 beading needle

Nymo beading thread, size D

Scissors

Dimensions: *28 inches (71 cm) long, not including pendant*

short links joining three rings

long link

FIGURE 1

The glass rings are linked with two types of links: long links and short links. Short links connect sets of 3 rings. Long links connect the sets of 3 to a single ring **(FIGURE 1)**.

Short Links

1 With ½ yard (45.5 cm) of single thread in the needle, work the following: Add 1 M, 1 A, and 1 M. Pass back through the first bead going toward the tail. Position the 3 beads so that they form a T and knot the thread to the tail **(FIGURE 2)**.

2 Add 1 M and pass through the third bead added in the previous step **(FIGURE 3)**.

3 *Add 1 A and pass through the previous bead **(FIGURE 4)**.

Add 1 M and pass through the previous bead 3 times.*

A (accent color)

M (main color)

FIGURE 2   **FIGURE 3**   **FIGURE 4**

4 Repeat from * to * until there are 8 A beads and 8 M beads alternating across the top row and 16 M beads in the bottom row. Your piece should look like **FIGURE 5**.

5 Work one row of brick stitch as follows: Turn the work so you are working left to right. Add 2 M. Pass the needle under the first thread bridge from back to front. Pass back up through the second bead added **(FIGURE 6)**.

6 Add 1 M. Pass under the next thread bridge, then back up through the bead just added **(FIGURE 7)**. This is 1 brick stitch.

7 Work 12 more brick stitches with M across the row. Increase 1 in the last loop **(FIGURE 8)**.

8 Joining Two Rings: Bring the 2 ends of the beaded strip through 2 rings. Zip the ends together as shown in **FIGURE 9**.

Then pass back and forth to reinforce the join. Knot the thread, weave in the tail, and clip.

9 Make another short link and join a third ring to the first 2 as described in step 8 **(FIGURE 10)**.

10 Make 6 sets of 3 rings.

Long Links (make 12)

Long links are made with single-needle ladder stitch 2 beads wide and brick stitch **(FIGURE 11)**.

1 Begin with 1½ yards (137 cm) of thread in your needle, single, leaving a 10-inch (25.5 cm) tail to join the link to the ring later. To work single-needle ladder, add 4 M and tie the thread to the tail so the beads form 2 columns parallel to each other. Pass through 2 beads **(FIGURE 12)**.

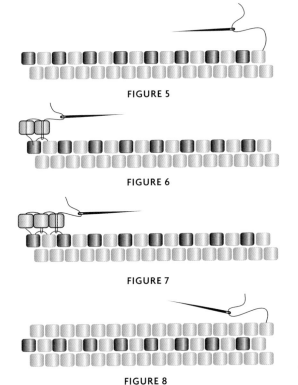

FIGURE 5

FIGURE 6

FIGURE 7

FIGURE 8

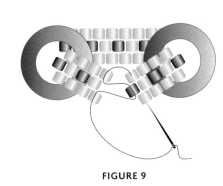

FIGURE 9

FIGURE 10

2 Add 2 M. Pass through the 2 previous beads from left to right, then through the 2 new beads from right to left **(FIGURE 13)**.

3 Add 2 M. Pass through the 2 previous beads from right to left, then through the 2 new beads from left to right **(FIGURE 14)**.

4 Continue until you have 12 pairs of M beads. The next pair will be 2 A, then continue the single-needle ladder with 9 pairs of M, 1 pair of A, and 1 pair of M.

5 Continue with brick stitch on the edge of the ladder. Turn the work so the thread is exiting the top of the bead on the left. Add 1 M and 1 A. Pass the needle under the second thread bridge from where it is exiting and pass back up through the second bead added **(FIGURE 15)**. To make the beads stand straight up, lock the stitch by going down through the first bead of the 2 added, then up through the second bead.

FIGURE 11

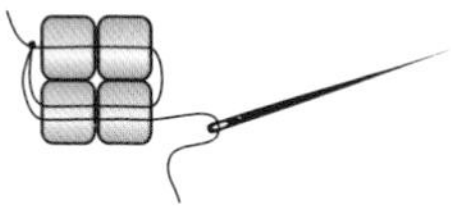

FIGURE 12

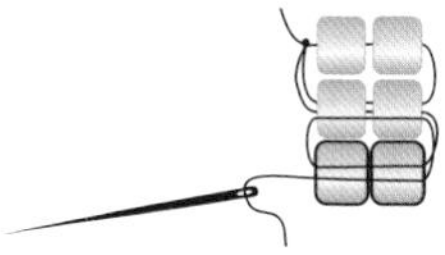

FIGURE 13

FIGURE 14

FIGURE 15

83

DIANE FITZGERALD'S FAVORITE BEADING PROJECTS

6 Continue across the row with brick stitch, adding 9 A and 1 M. Turn the work and work 11 M with brick stitch as described in step 5 of this section (FIGURE 16).

7 Pass your needle through to the first bead on the other side of the single-needle ladder and complete this side with brick stitch following the pattern above and steps 5 and 6 of this section (FIGURE 17). Pass thread through beads so it is exiting the first of the two beads added in step 1 of the Long Links.

8 Add 11 M with single-needle ladder (FIGURE 18).

9 Join one end to a single ring, continuing with the single-needle ladder technique and connecting as shown in FIGURE 19.

10 Join the other end to a set of 3 rings (FIGURE 20).

11 Continue to make long links and join them to single rings and sets of 3 rings as described on the picture on page 82.

FIGURE 16

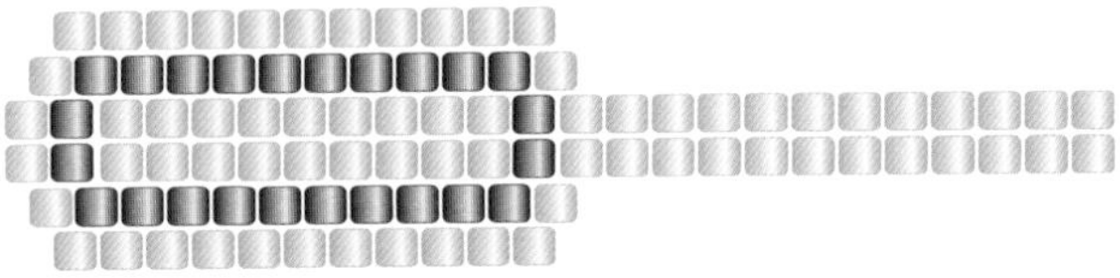

FIGURE 17

FIGURE 18

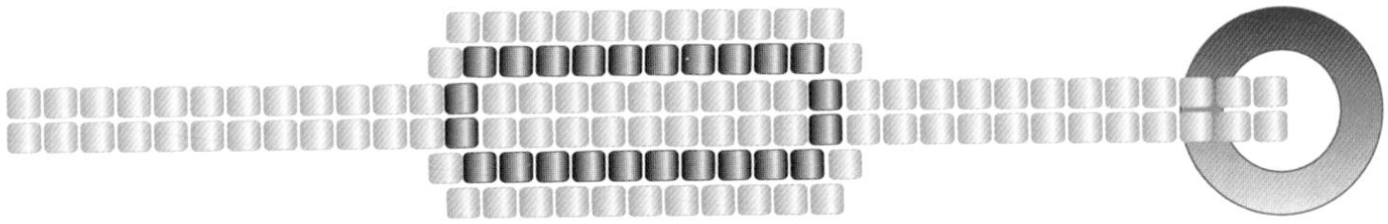

FIGURE 19

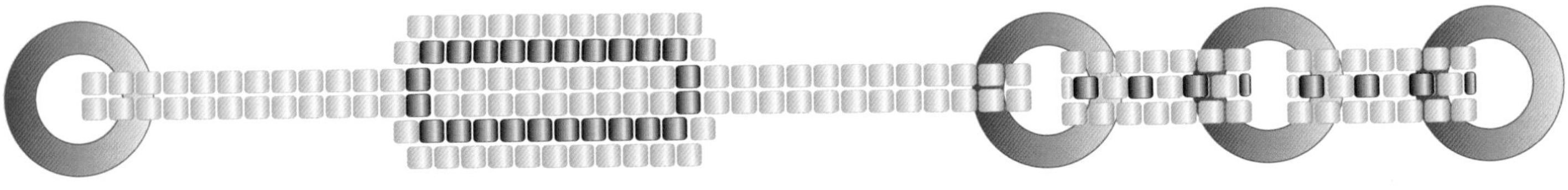

FIGURE 20

Pendant

The two-sided pendant is made of two pieces joined at the edges. Make the first side with brick stitch following the pattern in the diagram in **FIGURE 21**. Make the second side following the illustration in **FIGURE 22**. (Note that **FIGURE 21** is slightly wider than **FIGURE 22**.)

1 Thread the needle with 2 yards (2 m) of single thread. Directions are for **FIGURE 21**.

Row 1: Work single-needle ladder 1 bead tall by 8 beads wide as follows: String on 2 M and tie them into a loop, holding the work with the knot at the bottom **(FIGURE 23)**. Leave a 4-inch (10 cm) tail to hang on to, which will be woven in later.
Pass up through the bead on the right **(FIGURE 24)**.
Add 1 M. Pass up through the bead to the left, then down through the new bead just added **(FIGURE 25)**.

Add 1 M, then pass down through the previous bead and up through the new bead **(FIGURE 26)**.
Repeat the steps in Figures 25 and 26 until there are 8 beads across. Turn the work so your thread is exiting on the top left.

Row 2: Add 2 M. Pass the thread from back to front under the loop between the first and second beads of the previous row and back up through the last bead. This row extends beyond the beginning of the previous row **(FIGURE 27)**. Add 1 M. Pass the thread from back to front under the loop between the second and third beads of the previous row and back up through the last bead **(FIGURE 28)**. Continue to add 5 more brick stitches with M across the row. Increase in the last stitch by adding 1 M, passing under the last loop a second time, and then passing back up through the bead just added. There should be 9 M across the row.

Continue to work back and forth, following the pattern in **FIGURE 21**, and then make the back following the pattern in **FIGURE 22**.

2 Place the two pieces so the tops and bottoms are aligned; beginning at the top edge, work along the diagonal edge, joining the edges with square stitch **(FIGURE 29)**. Continue down the side, joining the edges by zipping them together. (The vertical edge beads of the front will be woven between the vertical edge beads of the back.) Whip stitch (see box) across the thread bridges at the bottom and continue on the other side in a similar manner.

whip stitch

Also known as overcast stitch, whip stitch is usually used to join two edges. With thread anchored in the fabric and holding the two edges aligned, pass the needle through both edges. Repeat for desired length.

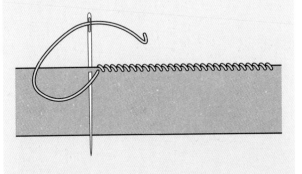

FIGURE 21

3 Before closing the top edge, cut out a rectangle of paper 1 x 1¾ inches (2.5 x 4.5 cm). Write your name, date, and location on it. If you wish, add a secret message on the back of the paper. Fold the paper in half and then in half again. Place it inside the pendant. Whip stitch the top edge closed.

4 Attach the pendant to a single ring that is between 2 long links, using 2 loops of 8 M beads. Add fringe by attaching a center strand with 15 M, a drop bead, and 1 M; make 2 side strands with 10 M, a drop bead, and 1 M **(FIGURE 30)**.

FIGURE 23

FIGURE 24

FIGURE 25

FIGURE 26

FIGURE 27

FIGURE 28

FIGURE 29

FIGURE 22

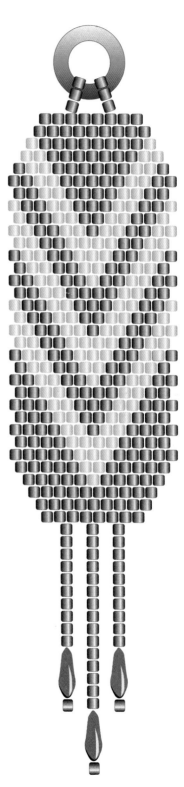

FIGURE 30

This simple yet delightful chain can be made any length. Although the instructions here are for a bracelet, you can bead a super-long chain instead and wear it many different ways as a necklace.

Diamond Chain

Bracelet

SUPPLIES

A, 88 crystal bicones, 4 mm

B, size 15° seed beads, 1 g

2 round metal beads, 3 mm

3 yards (2.7 m) of Fireline beading thread, 6 lb.

Size 12 beading needle

Microcrystalline wax

Clasp

Scissors

Disposable lighter

Dimensions: *7½ inches (19 cm) long*

1 Thread the needle, bring the ends together, wax the length of the thread well so that the strands adhere to each other like a single strand, knot the ends, and clip the tails 1 mm from the knot. Melt the ends with the lighter. (Don't put the tails in the flame, just near it.) Check to see that the knot is secure. Thread is used double because crystals have sharp edges.

2 Pass the thread through one half of the clasp to within 1 inch (2.5 cm) of the knot. Separate the strands between the clasp and knot. Pass the needle between the strands and pull up snug.

3 Add one 3 mm metal bead and 4 A. (Make sure the knot is tucked inside the 3 mm bead.) Pass back through the 3 mm bead, the clasp, and again through the 3 mm bead and the first A **(FIGURE 1)**.

FIGURE 1

FIGURE 2

FIGURE 3

FIGURE 4

4 Add 1 B. Pass through the next A. Repeat this step 2 more times. Pass through the first and second A (skipping the Bs), and end exiting the second B **(FIGURE 2)**.

5 Add 4 A. Pass through the B just exited again, turn the piece over, and pass through the first A **(FIGURE 3)**.

Add 1 B. Pass through the next A. Repeat this step 2 more times. Pass through the first 2 A (skip the Bs). End exiting the second B **(FIGURE 4)**.

6 Repeat step 5 for the desired length.

On the last repeat of step 5, instead of adding the second B, add a 3 mm round metal bead and the second half of the clasp. Pass back through the 3 mm round bead, then complete step 4 **(FIGURE 5)**. Knot, weave in the thread, and clip the tails.

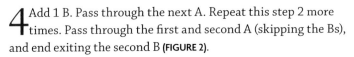
← knot

FIGURE 5

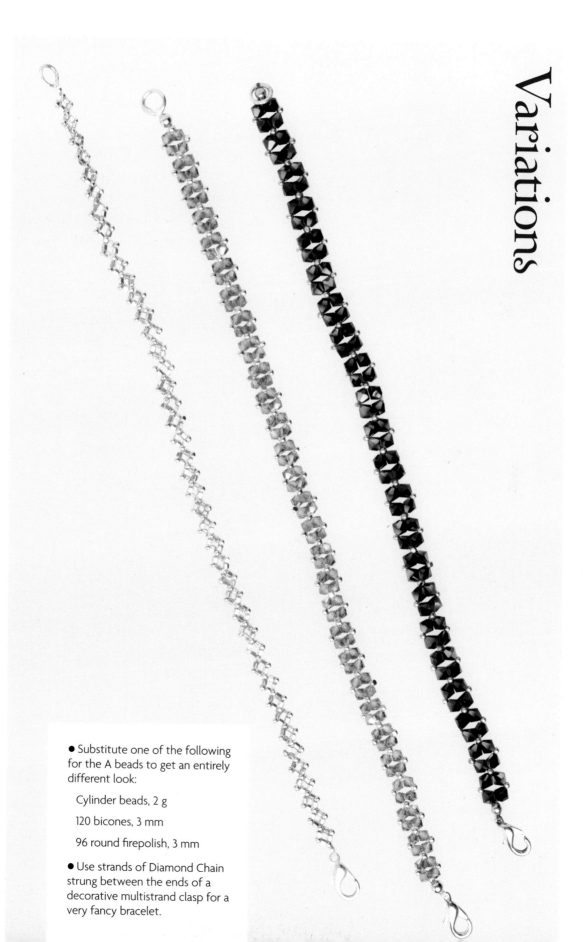

- Substitute one of the following for the A beads to get an entirely different look:

  Cylinder beads, 2 g

  120 bicones, 3 mm

  96 round firepolish, 3 mm

- Use strands of Diamond Chain strung between the ends of a decorative multistrand clasp for a very fancy bracelet.

This cheery little guy will make anyone smile. I carry one in my bead kit to keep me company when I'm traveling. My favorite parts are putting together the right buttons to shape the hat and drawing on the face with a happy smile.

button doll
ornament

SUPPLIES

54 assorted buttons, ½ to 2½ inches (1.3 to 6.5 cm) in diameter*

3 feet (91.5 cm) of 24-gauge craft wire

4 wood beads, 8 mm

1 wood bead, 25 mm

Red and black markers

10 inches (25.5 cm) of ribbon ¼ inch (6 mm) wide

Wire cutters

Ruler

*All buttons must have holes, rather than shanks. If you don't have a stash of old ones, plastic buttons in bright colors are available in craft stores. You can adjust the number and size of buttons as you wish.

Dimensions: *4¾ x 3⅛ inches (12 x 8 cm)*

1 Set aside the 4 largest buttons: 3 will be for the hat and 1 for the bottom of the torso. Cut 2 pieces of wire 12 inches (30.5 cm) long, and 2 pieces 6 inches (15 cm) long.

2 Make two legs. As you work steps 2 through 6, refer to **FIGURE 1**. String an 8 mm wood bead—which will be one of the Button Doll's feet—onto one of the 12-inch (30.5 cm) pieces of wire and position it in the center. Picking up 1 button, pass one end of the wire through one button hole and the other end through the opposite button hole. Add 10 more buttons to create a leg. Set aside and repeat to make the other leg.

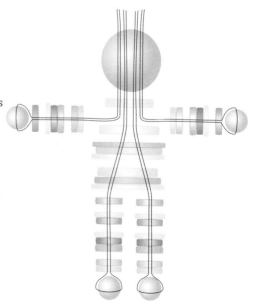

FIGURE 1

3 Make two arms. String an 8 mm wood bead—which will serve as one of the Button Doll's hands—onto one of the 6-inch (30.5 cm) pieces of wire and position it in the center. Picking up 1 button, pass one end of the wire through one button hole and the other end through the opposite button hole. Add 7 more buttons to create an arm. Set aside and repeat to make the other arm.

4 In this step, you'll make the torso, working from the bottom up. Using a 2½-inch (6.5 cm) button—or one of the larger buttons set aside in step 1—pass both wires from one leg through one button hole, then pass the other leg wires through the opposite hole. Add 8 more body buttons this way, gradually decreasing the size of the buttons.

5 Add 2 smaller-size buttons to the wires to create the neck as follows: Pass both wire ends of one arm and one leg through a button hole. Pass the

wire of the other arm and leg through the opposite hole in the button. Add a second button in the same manner.

6 Push all the buttons down tight, and twist the wires together a few times. Pass the wires through the 25 mm wood bead, then separate your wires again into 2 even sections.

7 You'll use the last 3 large buttons set aside in step 1 to make the hat. Pass one set of wires through the button hole of the largest button. Pass the other set of wires through the opposite hole. Repeat to add the 2 other buttons.

8 Twist all the wires together, then form a loop. Cut off any extra wire.

9 Use the markers to draw a face on the 25 mm wood bead.

10 Tie the ribbon around the wire ends and make a bow.

tag, you're it!

For an added touch, you may wish to add a tag made with shrink plastic with your name, a message, and the date. One Christmas, I made a whole slew of Button Dolls to give to my family as tree ornaments. My tag of white opaque shrink plastic said, "Merry Christmas! Love, Diane 2001." Even if you don't make a holiday label, do add the date to your little doll, so when someone finds this little figure in an antique store a hundred years from now, he or she will know just how old it is.

Merry Christmas!
Love
Diane

This elegant bracelet features a vintage button and is made with two simple stitches—brick stitch and square stitch—which combine to make strands resembling sinuous zippers.

Zipper Bracelet

SUPPLIES

A, matte navy blue AB size 8° hex beads, 12 g

B, cranberry AB size 8° hex beads, 10 g

C, bronze AB size 15° seed beads, 3 g

1 button with shank, ½ inch (1.3 cm) in diameter

Nymo nylon thread, size D, or Fireline thread, 6 lb.

Size 10 beading needle

Scissors

Microcrystalline wax

Dimensions: 1⅜ x 7⅝ inches (3.5 x 20 cm)

Make a Brick Stitch Triangle

Thread the needle with 3 yards (2.7 m) of thread. Bring the ends together and wax well so that the strands adhere to each other like a single strand. The thread is used double. Begin with the first 2 rows at the top of the triangle.

Make a brick stitch triangle for one end as follows **(FIGURE 1)**.

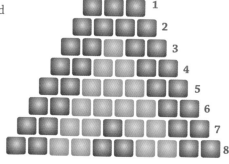

FIGURE 1

Rows 1 and 2: String 3 A. Pass back through the first bead in the opposite direction. Tie the thread to the tail, leaving a 3-inch (7.5 cm) tail to be woven in later. Make sure the beads form an inverted T (Rows 1 and 2 are worked at the same time; **(FIGURE 2)**.

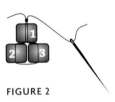

FIGURE 2

Add 1 A and pass through bead #3 **(FIGURE 3)**. Continue across the row following the pattern in **FIGURE 1**. You will be adding 3 A for Row 1 and 4 A for Row 2. Pass through to Row 2, exiting an end bead. Turn the work so the thread is exiting from the top left and you're working left to right.

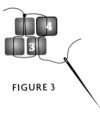

FIGURE 3

Row 3: (Brick Stitch) Add 2 A. Pass the needle from back to front under the thread bridge between the first and second beads of the previous row. Pass back through the last bead added. Continue across the row with brick stitch, following the color pattern in Figure 1. Increase at the end of the row by adding 1 extra A in the last thread bridge, passing under the same thread bridge as the previous stitch.

Rows 4–8: Continue working brick stitch following the pattern in **FIGURE 1** with increases at the end of each row.

Make the
Square Stitch Strands

Exiting the last bead in Row 8, add 2 A. Pass through the second A from the edge of the brick stitch triangle, then pass forward through the last bead of the base row and the new bead below it.

Continue Square Stitch: Add 2 A. Pass up through the bead next to the one the thread is exiting and add 1 C. Pass down through the bead next to it and through the first of the 2 new beads **(FIGURE 4)**.

Work the strand for 6¾ inches (17 cm), including the triangle (or until the piece is ¾ inch [2 cm] less than your wrist measurement). Knot the thread between the last 2 beads and weave in the tail.

Next strand: Anchor the thread so it is exiting the third bead in Row 8 of the triangle base and work square stitch with B and C like the first strand and to the same length.

Make the next strand with A and C, then one with B and C, then one with A and C.

Join the Strands and Make
the Second Triangle

Align the ends of the strands and join as shown in **FIGURE 5**. These beads will become the base row of the second triangle.

Work with decreasing brick stitch, following the color pattern in **FIGURE 1**. Decrease 1 bead per row by passing under the second thread bridge for the first stitch **(FIGURE 6)**. To make the first 2 beads of the row stand straight, "lock" the stitch as follows: Pass up through the second bead added, down through the first bead, and then back up through the second bead. Work until there's a row of 3 beads.

Attach a loop of C beads large enough to fit over the button, as shown in **FIGURE 7**.

Sew the button to the first triangle between the first and second rows.

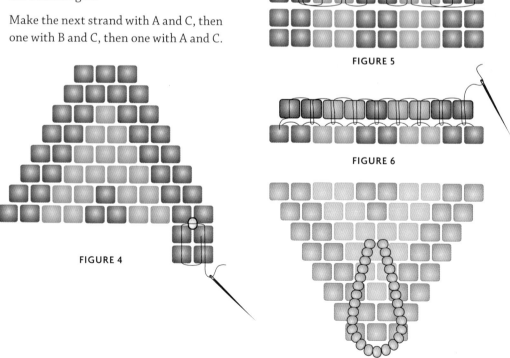

FIGURE 4

FIGURE 5

FIGURE 6

FIGURE 7

- Almost any beads can be used, including cylinder beads, cubes, or seed beads.

- The project can be made all in one color or with contrasting stripes.

- Add texture by mixing matte and shiny beads.

Braided
Garland
Necklace

Braided Garland Necklace

This necklace is made of five strands of wire strung with beads. Each strand also has beads twisted in place as short fringes spaced every ¾ to 1 inch (2 to 2.5 cm). The strands are then loosely braided using the five-strand method of braiding. The necklace has an adjustable chain closure.

SUPPLIES

2 accent beads, 12 mm

6 beads for the adjustable chain, 4 or 6 mm

Five 18-inch (45.5 cm) strands of beads*

15 yards (13.5 m) of 28-gauge wire

6 crimps (size 3 with an inner diameter of 1.5 mm) and 2 clamshell bead tips **or** 10 crimps, 2 eye pins (1½ inches [4 cm]), and 2 cones approximately ⅜ to ½ inch (1 to 1.3 cm)

Lobster-claw clasp and 1 closed ring or hook

7 eye pins and 1 head pin, 1 inch (2.5 cm) long, for the adjustable bead chain closure

Crimp covers to match the findings (optional)

Wire cutters

Needle-nose pliers

Round-nose pliers

Crimping tool

Macramé board or foam core board about 9 x 12 x½ inch (23 x 30.5 x 1.3 cm)

Straight pins

Tape measure or ruler

Tape

These can include any of the following beads: 3 or 4 mm firepolish or round glass beads up to 4 mm; pearls (check hole size); size 6°, 8°, or 11° seed beads; hex beads; or triangle beads. The beads may be all the same, or use 18 inches (45.5 cm) of each of 5 different beads. For each of the 5 strands of beads, you will need approximately 25 to 30 beads, which will be added like short strands of fringe to the wire base strand (referred to as fringe beads). These beads can be flower beads, leaves, loops of size 6° or 8° seed beads, petal beads, dagger beads, or whatever you wish. Color is probably more important than shape.

Dimensions: 18 inches (45.5 cm) long

Color: The Crucial First Decision

You may find it helpful to select a theme or an idea that you will express in your necklace. For example, an easy one would be autumn leaves. The color palette will be the autumn golds, reds, and greens. Look for leaves and other beads in these colors. It is especially important to have an accent color—in this palette, red, rusty red, carnelian, or gold might be the strongest colors. Then select beads that will be highlights and some that will give you some darker undertones.

Summer or spring flowers could be another appealing theme, and you will find many palettes of colors that work together. Look in magazines, flower books, craft stores that sell flower garland or berry branches, and elsewhere for ideas. If pastels are your choice, you should select colors that relate because they are light rather than vivid. Pale colors tend to blend, so you might want to add a strand of tiny silver or gold accents.

Another palette might be opaque bright beads for a summer theme. These colors will hold their own individually and won't tend to blend. Red and yellow will be the strongest colors, but be sure to add cobalt blues, deep purples, and greens to set them off.

Another interesting palette would be more muted whites, grays, and silver. Add a spark to this palette by including a deep garnet red bead.

Wire Color

Which to choose: gold, silver, or colored wire? There are many colors of wire available at craft and bead stores. Remember that the wire color will become a part of the design of your necklace. Gold warms your palette, silver cools it, and other colors could add or detract in various ways. Your wire color can blend or accent. Wire color, like thread color, should be the next decision after bead color.

Where to Start?

Make your first strand with the beads you feel are the strongest, most important, brightest, or whatever. Then work your remaining strands to complement this strand. To see how the beads will look, you may wish to make a few test strands without twisting in the fringe beads and then see how you like the effects. Also, if you complete a strand and later decide not to use it, rather than taking it apart, you might want to use it as the beginning of a new necklace.

Make the Strands

1 Cut the wire into 5 equal lengths, each 2½ yards (2.5 m) long. (Some lengths can be 2 yards [2 m] long if smaller fringe beads will be used.)

2 Beginning in the middle of a length of wire, add 1 fringe bead. Bring the wire along the back or side of the bead, cross the wire, and twist it 5 to 8 times **(FIGURE 1)**. The wire will be exposed on one side of the fringe bead. Working on either side of the wire, add about ¾ inch (2 cm) of strand beads and a fringe bead. Push into place within ¼ inch (6 mm) of the last strand bead, then twist the wire

to hold the fringe bead in place against the strand beads. Repeat until there are 9 inches (23 cm) of strand beads on the first side of the wire. Repeat for the other side of the wire so there's a total of 18 inches (45.5 cm) of strand beads and fringe beads, with ½ inch (1.3 cm) of only strand beads on each end. Use tape on the ends of the wire to keep the beads on. Leave any extra wire on the end for now and set aside.

3 Repeat this process for the remaining 4 strands of wire.

4 Position all 5 strands so that the first bead on each strand is next to the others. Pass all 5 wire ends through a crimp and push the crimp as close as possible to the beads **(FIGURE 2)**. Flatten the crimp with the crimping tool.

Braid

1 Pin the strands to the macramé board or foam core with straight pins. Beginning with the first strand on the right, pass it over the next strand to the left, under the next strand, over the next strand, and under the last strand. Arrange the strands after each sequence. Then repeat the process **(FIGURE 3)**.

2 As you work, keep the strands separated and untangled, and use pins to hold the braid in place if necessary. Bring the fringe beads to the front of the braid and position them as desired. After completing the braiding, add or remove strand beads so all strands are the same length, then pass all 5 wires through a crimp and flatten the crimp. Avoid removing fringe beads because the kinks that remain from twisting make it difficult to get the crimp on, and the wire may break if you attempt to straighten it.

3 If you have a special center bead, begin braiding in the middle of the braid. Align the centers of all strands with the center focal bead and braid one side, then the other, reversing the braiding pattern for the second half.

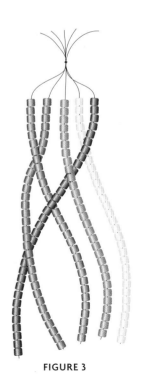

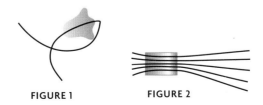

FIGURE 1   FIGURE 2   FIGURE 3

Finish and Add Findings

Two methods may be used to finish your necklace (instructions for both appear below). The first runs all the wires through 2 crimps, an accent bead, a crimp, a bead tip, and a third crimp. The second method uses a cone with each wire crimped to an eye pin that's inserted into the cone.

Method One

1 Add a second crimp bead and push it into place against the crimp already in place that joins the strands. Flatten the crimp. Make sure your wires are straight rather than twisted around each other, or the crimp may not fit over them **(FIGURE 4)**.

2 Add the accent bead to the 5 wires on one side. Add a crimp and flatten. Pass all strands through a clamshell bead tip. Add a crimp and flatten. Make sure the crimp is positioned parallel to the bead tip hinge so that it won't reopen when the bead tip is closed. Close the bead tip. Repeat the process on the other side.

3 On one side, add a jump ring and a lobster claw or hook closure.

4 On the other side, make a chain of eight 4 or 6 mm beads with eye pins and the head pin as follows: Insert the head pin so the plain end protrudes from the bead hole and clip it so that about ⅜ inch (1 cm) remains above the bead. Gripping the head pin just above the bead with the tip of the round-nose pliers, bend it at a right angle. Grip the end of the head pin and bend halfway around, then regrip and bend the remaining distance to form a loop. Open an eye pin and connect this unit to it. Close the eye pin. Add a 6 mm bead to the eye pin and make a loop on the other end as described for the head pin. Continue with the remaining four beads. Connect this chain to the bead tip.

Method Two

1 Pass one wire end through a crimp, then through the loop on the eye pin, then back through the crimp. Flatten the crimp to secure the wire **(FIGURE 5)**. Do this with the remaining 4 strands.

2 Pass the eye pin through the cone and attach your hook or lobster-claw clasp to one side and the bead chain to the other side as described in step 3 of Method 1.

Optional: Cover the crimps with crimp covers.

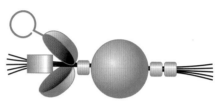

FIGURE 4

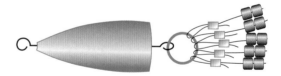

FIGURE 5

Sea Urchin
Necklace

Rings of dagger beads create the look of spiky sea urchins or flowers sewn to a cord base for a comfortable necklace that lies flat around your neck. A template of foam core board sized for your neck is used to sew and shape the cord base. The base is versatile because it can be embellished with many other types of beads, such as large resin beads, glass flowers, or buttons.

SUPPLIES

125 to 150 dagger beads, 5 x 16 mm

7 pearls, 6 mm

1 button, ⅝ inch (1.5 cm) in diameter

1 ¼yards (1.1 m) of round cord, ¼ inch (6 mm) in diameter*

Nymo beading thread, size D

4 inches (10 cm) of black ribbon, ⅝ inch (1.5 cm) wide

Size 10 beading needle

Microcrystalline wax

Disposable lighter

2 pieces of foam core board, 6 x 6 x ¼ inch (15 cm x 15 cm x 6 mm) and 8 x 10 x ¼ inch (20.5 cm x 25.5 cm x 6 mm)

Straight pins

Cutting blade

White tacky glue

*I use Wright's Basic #186-1173-031.

Dimensions: 1⅝ x 19¼ inches (4 x 49 cm)

Make the Template

The round template is used to create a necklace that lies just below the collarbone **(FIGURE 1)**. Templates are provided in 3 sizes: 16½ inches (42 cm), 17¼ inches (44 cm), and 18 inches (45.5 cm). Enlarge **FIGURE 1** 200%, trace the round template onto the smaller piece of foam core board, cut it out with a cutting blade, and glue it to the base of the larger foam core board using white glue. Draw a vertical center line on the round template. Round the corners of the base with the cutting blade. Position the round template in the center of the base, 1½ inches (4 cm) from the top edge. The completed template is shown in **PHOTO 1** (next page). The necklace may also be lengthened by cutting the round template in half and gluing down the 2 halves the necessary distance apart. For example, to increase the overall length by 1 inch (2.5 cm), place the 2 halves ½ inch (1.3 cm) apart.

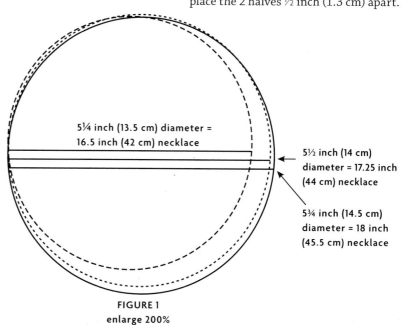

5¼ inch (13.5 cm) diameter = 16.5 inch (42 cm) necklace

5½ inch (14 cm) diameter = 17.25 inch (44 cm) necklace

5¾ inch (14.5 cm) diameter = 18 inch (45.5 cm) necklace

FIGURE 1
enlarge 200%

Prepare the Cord Base

Begin laying the cord around the template ¼ inch (6 mm) from the top center line as shown in **PHOTO 1** and **FIGURE 2**. Pass the cord around the template a little snug but without twisting. Pin it in place. At the top center line on the opposite side, fold the cord back ½ inch (1.3 cm) past the center line, then continue back around to meet the beginning end, but this time don't snug the cord. Fold the end to meet the beginning of the cord so that it overlaps the center line. Sew the ends together neatly. Cover the join with ribbon sewed in place. Sew ribbon around the cord on the buttonhole end also, for symmetry.

Sew the button to the top of the cord, ½ inch (1.3 cm) from the end. Continue stitching the 2 pieces of cord together in a zigzag pattern as shown. Stitch all the way through the center of both cords with each stitch, then backstitch to begin the next stitch. Reinforce the stitching ⅝ inch (1.5 cm) from the end for the buttonhole **(FIGURE 2)**.

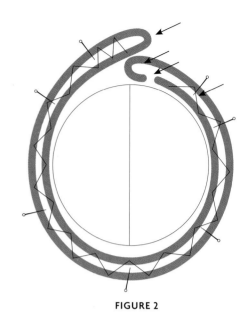

FIGURE 2

108

PHOTO 1

The template with the cord pinned in place, with a vertical center line drawn and a button waiting to be added.

Make Flowers

With 2 yards (1.8 m) of Nymo thread in your needle, bring the ends together, wax well so that the strands adhere to each other like a single strand, knot, clip the tails, and melt the ends with the lighter. (Don't put the tails in the flame, just near it.) Test the knot by pulling on the strands to make sure it's secure. String on the number of dagger beads according to the chart. Push the beads to within 1 inch (2.5 cm) of the knot, separate the strands between the beads and the knot, then pass the needle between the strands. Pass back through all the beads twice, pulling very tightly, knot, weave in the thread, and clip the tails.

Make 3 flowers with 13 beads.
Make 2 flowers with 11 beads.
Make 5 flowers with 10 beads.
Make 2 flowers with 9 beads.
Make 2 flowers with 8 beads.

Sew on the Flowers

Anchor the thread so it is exiting the center on the top of the completed cord base. Sew each flower on separately as follows: Pass the thread around the thread between the beads, then through the cord and up to the top again, like overcasting. Take a stitch after every bead. After working around the bottom flower layer, add the top flower layer on top of the first and sew it in place the same way (each flower has 2 layers). Add the round pearl to the flower center, stitching through it twice and placing it so the holes are on each side rather than the top.

Arrange the flowers with centers spaced 1¼ inches (3 cm) apart, as follows (the numbers indicate the number of daggers in each flower): Each flower is made of 2 rings of daggers with the lower ring larger than the top ring. For example, the center flower would have 13 daggers in the bottom ring and 10 daggers in the top ring.

number of petals in each flower layer

Bottom layer of daggers:	10	11	13	13	13	11	10
Top layer of daggers:		8	9	10	10	10	9	8

Variation

109

DIANE FITZGERALD'S FAVORITE BEADING PROJECTS

Embellish a cord base with almost any kind of beads, buttons, or charms for the look you want. This was a favorite type of bracelet created by Miriam Haskell in the 1930s.

Hard Candy
Bracelet

SUPPLIES

20 inches (51 cm) of round cord*, ¼ inch (6 mm) in diameter

Miscellaneous beads, buttons, seed beads, etc.

1 button, ½ to ⅝ inch (1.3 to 1.5 cm) in diameter

Nymo beading thread, size D

Size 10 beading needle

2 inches (5 cm) of black ribbon, ⅝ inch (1.5 cm) wide

Foam core board, 10 x 6 x ¼ inch (25.5 cm x 15 cm x 6 mm)

Straight pins

*I use Wright's Basic #186-1173-031.

Dimensions: 8¼ inches (21 cm) long

1 On the foam core board, mark a line 1 inch (2.5 cm) longer than your comfortable wrist measurement. Mark a line ½ inch (1.3 cm) from the left end of the line for the buttonhole loop, and a line ½ inch (1.3 cm) from the right end for the button placement.

2 Pin the cord to the board with the inner part of the fold on each end at the end of the line and cut the ends near the buttonhole loop. Join the ends by sewing **(FIGURE 1)**.

3 Sew on the button. Sew the 2 sides of the cord together, zigzagging back and forth as shown for the cord base in the Sea Urchin Necklace (page 106, **FIGURE 2**). Reinforce the sewing for the buttonhole loop. Sew a piece of ribbon over the join.

4 Sew on beads, buttons, or other embellishments, or even loops of size 11° seed beads if you wish. If you're adding dagger flowers, sew them 1 inch (2.5 cm) apart.

FIGURE 1

Variations

Front

Back

For a wider bracelet base, begin with 40 inches (101.5 cm) of round
cord and pin 2 pairs of cord to the foam core board template.

Knotty
Necklace

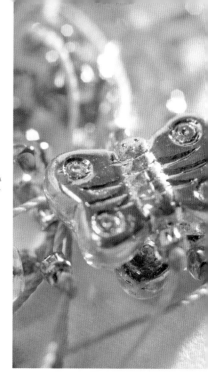

Knotty Necklace

This lightweight multistrand necklace lets you explore the possibilities of fiber, with knots to hold the beads in place. Beaded strands may be finished with a spiraling knot, braided, or even made into a single, extra long continuous strand.

SUPPLIES

12 yards (11 m) of nylon cord (Conso #18*, size FF or FFF bead cord)

2 large accent beads**

40 beads, 8 to 10 mm

48 beads, 4 to 5 mm, or size 8° seed beads

150 to 200 size 11° seed beads

Clasp (optional)

Scissors

Clear nail polish or watch crystal cement

Macramé board or foam core board, 8 x 10 x ½ inch (20 x 25 x 1.3 cm)

Scissors

7 T-pins and work surface

Large needle

Conso #18 cord is a smooth, heavy nylon cord found in fabric and upholstery shops. FF and FFF bead cord is similar and is available in bead stores. Both come in a variety of colors.

**The holes should be large enough to pass 8 strands of bead cord through, or if necessary, only 4 strands*

Dimensions: *23⅝ inches (60 cm) long*

1 Cut 8 pieces of cord, each 1½ yards (1.4 m) long. Make an overhand knot in the middle of 1 of the cords. String on 1 seed bead, 1 larger bead, and 1 seed bead, or any other arrangement. Make another overhand knot, placing it so it holds the beads tightly in place against the previous knot.

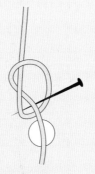

FIGURE 1

placing and tightening an overhand knot

To make an overhand knot, hold the cord in your left hand. Pass one end of the cord over the cord in your hand, forming a loop. Pass the end of the cord through the loop. To control the placement of an overhand knot so it's tight against a bead, make the knot, then place a pin in the loop before tightening. Push the pin next to the bead, then pull on the end of the cord **(FIGURE 1)**.

2 Work the right side of the cord, as follows: Tie another knot approximately 1 inch (2.5 cm) to the right of the first bead. Add 1 seed bead, 1 smaller bead, and 1 seed bead, and knot to hold them in place. Continue to alternate larger beads and smaller beads with seed beads on both sides until you have 3 larger beads and 3 smaller beads on the right side of the cord.

3 For the left side of the cord, flip the cord and repeat step 2.

4 Make 8 strands similar to this. Your beads may be different and you may wish to arrange them differently. For example, you may wish to begin with a small bead in the center instead of a large one on some strands or you may decide to not place a bead in the center.

5 Lay out all strands with their center points aligned. Gather all the strands together and knot the ends together on one side, ½ to 1 inch (1.3 to 2.5 cm) from the last beads. Repeat for the other side. Coat the ends with clear nail polish and allow them to dry before stringing.

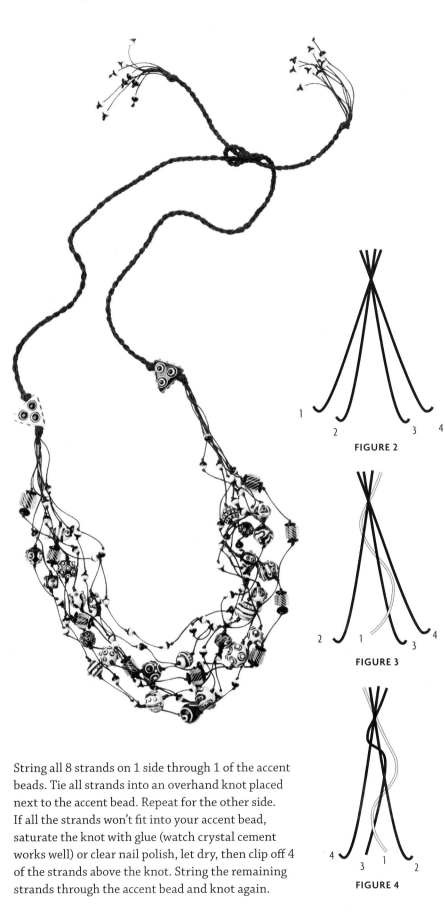

Finish
Option 1: Braid the Ends

Braid the 8 strands into a 4-strand braid 10 to 12 inches (25.5 to 30.5 cm) long on each side.

The braid is done in a 2-step process, first working from the left, then from the right. With the knot in the strands pinned to the macramé board, fan the 8 strands out in front of you so you have 4 pairs, and consider each pair as 1 strand **(FIGURE 2)**.

1 Beginning on the left, pass the outermost strand (#1), under #2 and #3, then back over #3 toward the left **(FIGURE 3)**. (This is the left side step of the braid.)

2 Counting from the right, pass the outermost strand on the right under #2 and #3 and back over #3 **(FIGURE 4)**.

3 Repeat steps 1 and 2 on both sides of the necklace until 1½ to 2 inches (4 to 5 cm) of cords remain. Finish the ends by knotting all strands of the braid into a single overhand knot, leaving about 1½ inches (4 cm) unbraided. Finish the ends with a smaller bead, then a seed bead and an overhand knot. Dab the knot with clear nail polish or watch crystal cement. To secure the necklace, tie it around your neck with a square knot.

FIGURE 2

FIGURE 3

FIGURE 4

String all 8 strands on 1 side through 1 of the accent beads. Tie all strands into an overhand knot placed next to the accent bead. Repeat for the other side. If all the strands won't fit into your accent bead, saturate the knot with glue (watch crystal cement works well) or clear nail polish, let dry, then clip off 4 of the strands above the knot. String the remaining strands through the accent bead and knot again.

115

Option 2: Spiraling Half-Knots

This simple macramé knot is quick to do once you get the hang of it. The same knot is worked for the length desired, then a clasp is added.

After you've completed the multistrand portion and knotted the strands together (with or without the accent bead), begin the half-knots. Pin the work to a macramé or foam core board. Loosely tie 6 of the cords together near the end (these will be your base cords) and leave 2 of the cords free. These will be your knotting cords. Position 1 of the knotting cords to the left of the base cords and 1 to the right.

Optional: For a thicker spiral, use only 4 cords for the base cords and 2 cords for each of the left and right knotting cords instead of 1 for each.

1 Pass the left cord over the base cords **(FIGURE 5)**.

2 Pass the right cord over the left cord and behind the base cords **(FIGURE 6)**.

3 Pass the right cord over the left cord again, then through the loop to exit behind the left cord **(FIGURE 7)**. Pull tight, and repeat for desired length.

116

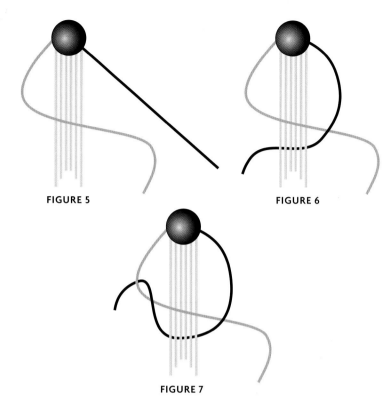

FIGURE 5

FIGURE 6

FIGURE 7

tip

Keep the knotting pinned to the board in several places. When pulling to tighten the knot, make sure the base cords are straight and pull on the left and right cords at right angles to the base cords. When the knotting is within ½ inch (1.3 cm) of the desired finished length, usually 4 to 6 inches (10 to 15 cm), bring the base cords through 1 side of the clasp and fold them back. Continuing with the left and right cords, continue knotting to the clasp. Place a dot of glue (watch crystal cement is recommended) on the last few knots. Weave in the left and right cords with a large needle and clip all ends close to the knotting.

SUPPLIES

45 to 50 larger beads, 6 to 10 mm

100 seed beads

4 yards (3.7 m) of nylon cord, size FF, FFF, or #18

Variation: Continuous Loop Knotty Necklace

This necklace can be worn in a number of ways—looped twice around your neck; looped three times around your neck; folded in half and in half again and twisted and secured around your neck with a ring closure; or folded in half three times and worn as a bracelet with a ring closure.

Knot the cord with an overhand knot **(FIGURE 1)** 6 inches (15 cm) from the end. Add 1 seed bead, 1 larger bead, and 1 seed bead. Knot the cord again so the knot holds the beads tight against the previous knot. Place the next knot 1 to 1½ inches (2.5 to 4 cm) along the cord, depending on the size of your larger beads. Each unit of knot, seed bead, larger bead, seed bead, and knot should be about 1½ inches (4 cm) long. Continue to add these units until the string measures 72 to 84 inches (1.8 to 2.1 m). Knot the ends together with a square knot, pass both strands through the last bead, do the first half of a square knot, then pass the ends around the cord and do a complete square knot. Saturate the knot with glue. Clip the ends. (After passing the ends through the last bead, you could also glue the ends in place with watch crystal cement.)

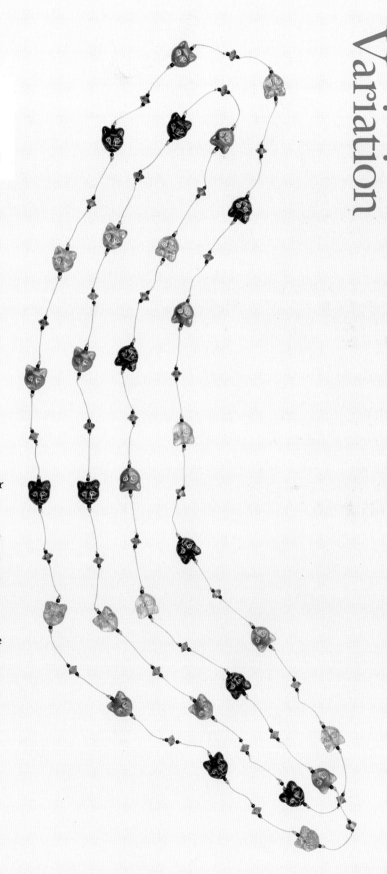

117

Canterbury Necklace

Canterbury Necklace

In Renaissance Europe and again in Victorian England, a type of necklace known as a carcanet, or jeweled collar, was all the rage. My carcanet design is made of small, square tabular pieces that are strung together. They're made with peyote stitch, to which trimmings are added. The fun part of this necklace is collecting the embellishments! Tiny buttons, margaritas, chatons, nailheads, flat pressed leaf or flower beads, or beaded shapes may be used. The tabular pieces may also be strung as a bracelet.

120

SUPPLIES

Size 11° light bronze metallic cylinder beads, 30 g

Embellishments*

24 rondelles, 4 mm

Nymo beading thread, size D, to match the cylinder beads

Microcrystalline wax

Size 10 beading needle

28 inches (71 cm) of beading wire

2 crimp beads

Clasp

Crimping pliers

*Rose montées, tiny buttons, flat beads, nail-heads, leaves, flowers, margaritas, chatons, etc.

Dimensions: 17¾ inches (45 cm) long

Bead a Tab

Each tab is made with flat peyote, so this is a great project for beginners learning the stitch. Tabs are ⅝ x ⅝ inch (1.5 x 1.5 cm). Each tab is 12 beads wide and 40 rows long, and there are 23 tabs in the pictured necklace. In the illustrations below, new beads are shown with a bold outline. Work with medium to soft tension so it's easier to sew on embellishments later.

Even-Count Flat Peyote Stitch

Thread the needle with 1 yard (91.5 cm) of thread and wax it well. String on a stopper bead and pass through this bead again in the same direction as the first pass. This bead will be removed later.

Row 1: String on 12 cylinder beads (FIGURE 1).

Row 2: Add 1 cylinder bead and pass through the third bead from the needle end going toward the stopper bead (FIGURE 2).

Continue to work across the row, adding 1 bead, skipping the next bead, and passing through the second bead from where your thread exited a bead. You'll be adding 6 beads across the row (FIGURE 3). Remove the stopper bead and tie the working thread to the tail.

Row 3: Add 1 cylinder bead and pass through the last bead added in the previous row.

Continue to work across the row, adding 1 bead, skipping the next bead, and passing through the second bead from where your thread exited a bead. You'll add 6 beads across the row (FIGURE 4).

FIGURE 1

FIGURE 2

Rows 4–20: Continue working rows back and forth as you did for Rows 2 and 3.

After working a few rows, weave the beginning end of the thread through several beads and clip the tail.

How to Count Rows

When adding the beads for Row 1, you are actually adding the first 2 rows of beads.

To count the number of rows, count the beads along the right edge: 1, 3, 5, 7, etc., and on the left edge: 2, 4, 6, 8, etc. **(FIGURE 5)**.

Form the Tab

To form the tab, join the beginning edge to the last row, Row 40. This process is called zipping because you're joining the edges, which are like the teeth of a zipper **(FIGURE 6)**.

Fold the strip so the edges are aligned, with "up" beads on one end fitting between the "up" beads on the other end.

After zipping the edges together, you have a tube that will be flattened.

To form a channel for the beading wire, pass through to the edge and stitch the edges of the tube together on both the left and the right edges, 3 beads from the fold **(FIGURE 7)**.

To sew your element to the flattened tube, position the element on the flat side and stitch through the beads or between the beads to anchor the element.

Finish

Embellish the tab as desired.

Make as many tabs as you wish. Since you'll string the tabs onto beading wire, you can make the necklace longer or shorter to suit your taste.

To assemble the necklace, string on a crimp and one half of the clasp, then pass back through the crimp and flatten it with crimping pliers. String on 1 rondelle and then alternate tabs and rondelles, ending with a rondelle. Add the second crimp and the second half of the clasp, then pass back through the crimp and flatten it. If you wish, string the tabs as you make them; this allows you to begin wearing the necklace as soon as you complete the first tab.

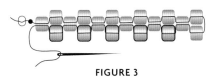

FIGURE 3

FIGURE 4

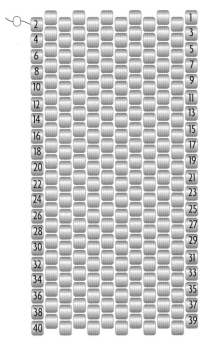

FIGURE 5

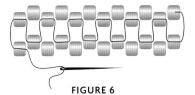

FIGURE 6

FIGURE 7

121

122

Shaped Tila Bead Necklace, 2010

PENDANT, 16.5 X 13 CM

TILA BEADS, DROP PENDANTS, CHAIN; SQUARE STITCH

This is a shaped necklace made with the new Tila beads from Miyuki Co. of Japan. The beads are 5 x 5-mm squares with two holes and they make a fabulous fabric of beads. The shape of the design was inspired by an earlier design that I made for my book *Beads and Threads: A New Technique for Fiber Jewelry*, co-authored with Helen Banes.

Amazon Feather
Necklace, 2005

38 X 61 CM

MIYUKI DELICA BEADS, FEATHERS, LEATHER; BRICK STITCHED, GLUED

The brightly colored feathers of Amazon featherwork and the geometric patterns in their weaving inspired this broad collar. The black and white seed bead panels provide a sharp contrast in shape, color, and scale to the orange and green dyed feathers. The piece was made for a beading group challenge focusing on large collar neck pieces.

123

Amazon Feather
Cuff, 1995

6.5 X 21 X 1.5 CM

DELICA BEADS, FEATHERS, SEEDS; PEYOTE STITCH

This cuff, with its cluster of seedpods and fluffy feathers placed against a background of spiral diamonds, was also inspired by native South American featherwork.

Personal Symbols Necklace, *2005*

62 X 2.5 CM

CYLINDER BEADS; DIAGONAL BRICK STITCH

Shapes, lines, and bright colors come together in this design, which is worked without a pattern.

Bead Pal Necklace, *2010*

63 CM LONG

SEED BEADS; OFF-LOOM BEADING STITCH

This was a project cooked up one evening by Stephney Hornblow and me. We decided it would be fun if 12 British beaders and 12 American beaders paired up and did a "hands across the water" project. We each made 12 beads for our bead pal and 12 for ourselves. Any beads could be used, but colors were limited to cream, copper, and black so the necklace would look unified when strung.

Tulip Pouch Necklace, 2001

24 X 15 CM

BEADS, CHARMS, FABRIC; NETTING

Victorians often carried small, netted pouches to hold their coins or keys. The pouch shape and use of netting inspired this version, which can be worn as a pendant necklace. It's accented with American art glass beads.

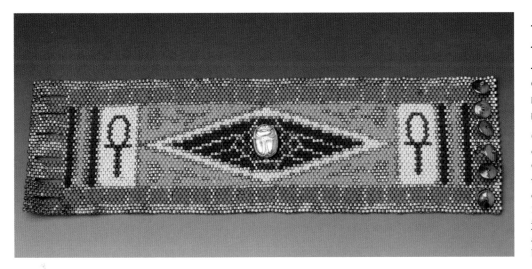

Egyptian Motif Peyote Bracelet, 2002

6 X 20.5 CM

DELICAS, SCARAB BEAD; PEYOTE STITCH

Occasionally, I offer an extended class on a special theme in the Twin Cities area. In one of these classes, we looked to ancient Egyptian designs for our inspiration. I collect 1920s Egyptian Revival costume jewelry, which seems to incorporate an endless variety of pressed glass beads and pendants.

126

Rose Garden
Necklace, 2000

PENDANT, 7 X 15 X 1.5 CM

SEED BEADS; PEYOTE STITCH, NETTING

Beaded flowers—with thread instead of
wire—are one of my passions, and these
flowers are one of the many designs I
created for my book *The Beaded Garden*.

Tongue Bead Chain, 1999

51 CM LONG

**SEED BEADS, PRESSED GLASS
TWO-HOLE BEADS; NETTING**

This is an unusual chain made with oval
two-hole beads and "tongue" beads
re-created from a necklace a friend was
repairing. Surprisingly, the same beadweaving techniques used with regular beads can
be used to connect two-hole beads.

Acknowledgments

Writing a book and bringing it through to publication is, in many ways, like giving birth to a child; you experience both the enjoyment of creation and the pain of delivery. But it's like bringing a child into the world in other ways as well. An author is never sure what the new "child" will be like, its strengths and weaknesses, how it will be received, whether it will be liked or not, famous or infamous. Another important similarity is that one rarely does it alone. In the case of this book, many along the way helped. First, my students across the country who for the last 20 years took my classes and worked through the instructions to create beautiful beadwork, suggested ways of saying things, and found the inevitable errors. To all of you, my heartfelt thanks.

Next, my thanks go to Bonnie Brooks, the technical editor, and J'aime Allene, the illustrator; the staff of Lark Jewelry & Beading who make the books they publish so spectacular, including Kathleen Holmes, the art director; Carol Morse Barnao, junior designer; Melissa Morrisey, art intern; and Abby Haffelt, whose meticulous attention to detail helped so much. Thanks, too, to Lynne Harty, the photographer, and Pamela Norman, the book and cover designer. Most of all, I wish to thank Nathalie Mornu, my trusted editor, for her attention to detail, her respect of my wishes, and her most pleasant attitude throughout the process. I could not imagine a better editor.

Of course, my dear hubby deserves a little credit too, for all the times he's patient with me when I'm tense as a deadline looms.

PHOTO BY MICHAEL MALLOY

About the Author

In a beading career spanning more than 20 years, Diane Fitzgerald has studied both historical and contemporary beadwork and applied what she's learned to teaching across the United States and internationally. Diane is the recipient of the 2011 Spun Gold Award from the Textile Center of Minnesota, a recognition based on significant contributions to the field of fiber art. She's also a 2012 Designer of the Year for *Beadwork* magazine and a Swarovski Ambassador. She has written 10 other books and numerous magazine articles.

Diane believes sharing our creations makes them all the more meaningful and satisfying. She encourages you to write her with any questions and, if you wish, to send her images of your finished pieces. Email her at dmfbeads@bitstream.net.

Index